Live to Love, Love to Live
A Manual on Living and Loving

Note: Quoted verses are from the *New American Catholic Bible*.

Live to Love, Love to Live
A Manual on Living and Loving

by
Medardo Gonzales

SUNSTONE
PRESS

SANTA FE

No part of this book may be reproduced in any form or by any electronic or mechanical means including
information storage and retrieval systems without permission in writing from the publisher, except by a reviewer who may quote brief passages in a review.

Sunstone books may be purchased for educational, business, or sales promotional use. For information please write: Special Markets Department, Sunstone Press, P.O. Box 2321, Santa Fe, New Mexico 87504-2321.

Book and cover design › L.R. Ahl
Printed on acid-free paper
∞

Library of Congress Cataloging-in-Publication Data

(ON FILE)

~Dedication

This book is dedicated to Almighty God, Father, Son, and Holy Spirit in thanks giving for all his blessings, honor and glory and without whose help it would have been impossible to write. It was the Holy Spirit who guided me, inspired me, and motivated me to write this book as a labor of love and thanksgiving to him in whom we have our being, our life, joy, peace, and salvation. I also want to thank my family, all eight children, twenty-seven grandchildren, and close to fifty great-grand-children for their love, patience, and encouragement in the writing of this book. And a special thanks goes to their mother, Jennie, for always believing in me.

Contents

Introduction

What has Love got to do with it? An interesting question, no? Are you totally, happily, lovingly and completely satisfied with the way your life is going? If you're not, or if you want to know more about life and love, you have picked the right book to read. In order to live a joyful, peaceful, and loving life with one's self and with others we must first learn to let go of old, negative attitudes and habits that are inhibiting our ability to love and learn and practice positive and loving attitudes and habits that will bring joy, peace, patience, kindness, faithfulness, goodness, gentleness and self-control into our lives.

This book is based on precepts given to us by none other than The Great Author of Life Himself, Almighty God through His Son, Jesus Christ, who saved me from a life of stinky thinkin' and actin', and who taught me how to truly love. He is ready to do the same for you. Because He gave His life for our sins, and because He loves us so much, Jesus reaches out to us throughout the Old and New Testaments to repent, turn away from sin and to love one another as He loves us.

This is not another manual on love, marriage or interpersonal relationships but rather a guide to loving oneself which in turn leads us to love, first God, than others as we love ourselves, for it is impossible to love others unless we love ourselves first. And it is impossible to love ourselves as God loves us unless we love God with all our hearts, with all our minds, and with all our souls for God is Love. Almost everything that is written herein is taken from Holy Scripture. It is the author's belief that, although written by men and women inspired by God down through the ages, all Holy Scripture is dictated by Almighty God himself and is therefore infallible, for God is the same then, now and forever. He is the Alpha and the Omega, the Beginning and the End, who is and who was, and who is to come; the Almighty. (Revelations1: 8)

In case you're wondering whether this is a history of the human species, it is not. Science tells us that the human species existed at least 200,000 years ago and gradually spread throughout the world. Science does not tell us who the first humans to be created out of the dust were, and their roles in God's Plan. That is why the *Bible* was dictated to Man by God. What we are concerned with is with the creation of the first humans, Adam and Eve, why they (and we) were created, what God expected to happen after they were created, what happened after they sinned, how that affected the rest of humanity, and how God saved the world from sin, and what our roles are in the God's Plan for us.

How to Use This Book.

This book is divided into five parts: The first part explains what love is and the different kinds of love or stages of love there are and how we go through each stage until we reach the Agape stage, or God's Love. The second part is the story of God's love for us, how He created the world, why He created the world and humans, and what His plan of salvation is. This part is based on the Old Testament. In the third part God reveals His Plan of Salvation and what we must do to be saved. In this part also we learn how He expects us to love one another in order to be saved. In the fourth and fifth parts, we will discover how to live to love and love to live, and what will happen at the end of the world when Jesus comes back to take His Elect into His Glorious home, and what will happen to those who don't deserve eternal salvation.

Part One

1 ~ Definition of Love:

What is love? Is it a feeling, an emotion, an attitude, a state of being, a desire? It is all of these and more. It has been described in many different ways. It has been described as Spectacular, Powerful, Many Splendored, Joyful, Hurtful, Ecstatic, Spiritual, Liking, Friendly, Unconditional, Sacrificial, Intense, Undying, Caring, Giving, Euphoric, Trusting, Passionate, Joyful, Patient, Kind, Forbearing, Unending and a host of other things, including the act of sex between a man and a woman.

The word "love" has been used to describe so many different acts, feelings, ways of doing certain things and emotions that it is sometimes difficult to know what exactly is meant by the word, love. For example, we can tell someone we love their house or their teeth, or that we love going to a certain restaurant, that we love our dog or that we love that person or that make of car, etc. Get it? We use the word love as a noun, a verb, an adjective or to describe sexual acts. No wonder people get confused.

Thousands of books have been written on the subject of love but in this book, we are concerned only with the kind of love that exists between God, Man, and each other, and that covers the four different kinds of love instituted by God Himself: Eros, Storges, Phileo, and the highest form of love, Agape Love, or Total Love, the way God loves us, and has loved Man since He created him. Agape Love is described in the *Bible* in John 3: 16, often called "The Gospel In A Nutshell" because it is considered a summary of what Christianity is all about and is often the most quoted verse in scripture when describing God's Love for us. The words Eros, Storges, Phileo and Agape are Greek words and you won't find them in English *Bibles*, but their meanings are found in both the Old and the New Testaments in any language. All we know for sure is that Love is of God because God is Love. (1 John 4: 7, 8)

The Apostle Paul in 1 Corinthians 13, in part, describes love in this way: "Love is patient; love is kind; love is never envious. Love is never boastful, nor conceited, nor selfish. Love is never rude. It is not prone to anger; neither does it brood over injuries. Love does not seek revenge; neither does it rejoice in what is wrong but rejoices with the truth. There is no limit to love's forbearance, to its trust, its hope, its power to endure. Love never fails. In the end, there are three things that last forever: faith, hope and love; but the greatest of these is love." This is called Agape Love and is the kind of love we are mostly concerned with in this book.

Chapter 13: 1-3 of 1 Corinthians also tells us that even if we possess all the gifts of the Holy Spirit, we are nothing but a clanging cymbal or a noisy gong, unless we have love. In other words, all our talk about being good Christians and loving God is nothing unless we possess, and practice, all the attributes of Agape love towards one another. (See also 1 John 4: 7-13, 16-31)

Kinds of Love

The four kinds or types of love which we are concerned with in this book are briefly described below.

1. EROS: Erotic, Sexual or Romantic Love. This kind or type of love, which is named after the Greek goddess of love and fertility, is based on physical attraction, sexual desire, and feelings of tenderness and wanting to share, such as those that exist between husband and wife, sweethearts, and even friends. When you "eros" love someone, you may first be attracted to them in a physical way, such as their looks, their personalities, or other attributes. An attraction of this kind may lead to dating, friendship, physical intimacy and eventually even to marriage. Even though the term "eros" is not found in the *Bible*, *The Song of Solomon* or *The Song of Songs* in the Old Testament, vividly portrays the passion of erotic love. The *Bible*, which is the Word of the Lord, is very clear that erotic love, which God made both enjoyable and for a specific purpose, is reserved for males and females for the propagation of the species and for the enjoyment of the man and woman. (see Genesis 1: 22 and 28)

God created man and woman which He created in His image, and the first humans He created were named Adam and Eve. When you think Eros, think Valentine's Day. While all kinds of love come from God, erotic Love is different from the others in that it was made to be for the propagation of the human race and therefore to be enjoyed.

Although God created heterosexuals for the propagation of the human race, He created homosexuals and lesbians as well and He wants us to agape love them just like He loves them, too. This is something that only God understands, and we are not to judge them, only to love them as brothers and sisters.

Have you ever wondered why God created so many different races and colors of people in so many different shapes and sizes and features? Have you ever wondered why no two human beings are exactly alike or why no set of fingerprints are the same match to any other set of fingerprints? I believe God created such diversity in the human condition so that we may love each and every human being equally as He does no matter what size, shape, color, condition or sexual orientation they are. Did not Jesus say, "You shall love the Lord, your God with your whole heart, your whole soul and with all your mind and your neighbor as yourself"? And who is our neighbor? Every human being we come in contact with is our neighbor and we, straights, homosexuals, Blacks, Whites, Browns, Purples, whatever color, shape or form, are all created equal in the image, or as a reflection, of God. But getting back to the Eros kind of love, while most relationships usually start out in the Erotic stage, they may, especially if a couple marry, move on into the Storge and the Agape stages of Biblical Love. And it is possible to experience all four types of love with the same person, especially one you are married to or living with, at the same time!

2. STORGE OR FAMILIAL LOVE. Storge Love is family love. It is a bond of love that exists between husband and wife, parents, siblings, grandparents, close friends and kin, such as aunts, uncles, and cousins. It is based on deep friendship, kinship and relationship. The *Enhanced Strong's Lexicon,* describes, Storge Love, in part, as "cherishing one's kindred, especially parents, or children; the mutual love of parents and children and wives and husbands..." This is also the kind of love that God, the Father has had for His Only Begotten Son, Jesus, and for the Holy Spirit and the kind of love Jesus and the Holy Spirit have had for the Father; and for each other, and this is the kind of love that Almighty God, our Triune God who is made up of One deity in three divine entities Father, Son and Holy Spirit. and the kind of love he has for us humans, who by virtue of being descendants of Adam and Eve, are his creation, or His children, too. That makes us all members of God's family.

3. PHILEO OR BROTHERLY LOVE. Phileo, or brotherly love is the kind of love that Jesus wants us to have for one another. It is the kind of love that He had for his apostles and disciples and all whom He came in contact with and the kind of love that Jesus commands us to have for others, even our enemies. Phileo, along with Storge and Agape, love is what Jesus has for those who love Him, who believe in Him, and who obey His commandments and who love one another as themselves. So Brotherly Love is what we, too, ought to have for God, our own selves, and others, even our enemies (except Satan who is The Enemy). If God has this kind of love for us, and parents have this kind of love for their spouses, their parents, and their offspring, and children have the same kind of love for their parents, grandparents and siblings, shouldn't we all have the same kind of love for each other?

4. AGAPE LOVE. Agape Love is the highest form of Love. It is God Love; it is the love of Jesus Himself. It is love at its ultimate. It is a self-sacrificing love, the kind of love that God has for all humans; the kind of love Jesus poured out for us sinners when He took our sins upon Himself and died on the cross for us; this is the kind of love we see when someone sacrifices themselves for the love of God and others, such as when a soldier jumps on top of a live grenade to save the lives of his comrades; or the act of a stranger who jumps in front of a speeding car and pushes a child out of the way and dies in the act of saving the life of the child.

Christ died so that our sins could be forgiven, and we could be with Him in heaven for eternity. Even His last words on the Cross were love words uttered on behalf of us sinners, when He said, "Father forgive them for they know not what they do!" (Luke 23: 34) When He said these words, He wasn't just talking about the Roman soldiers who abused and crucified Him and the Jewish priests who condemned Him to death, but also about the past, present, and future sinners for whom He was offering His life. In other words, He took our sin upon Himself. He who was without sin, took our sins upon His Holy Body so that we might have eternal life. In John 3: 16 it is written that, "God so loved the world that He gave His only begotten Son that whoever believes in Him shall not perish but have everlasting life." Oh, what a glorious day that will be! I can hardly wait! It stands to reason that Agape Love is the highest and purest form of love for "God Is Love." (1 John 4: 8)

Part Two

2 ~ Angels, Cherubim and Seraphim

During our study of how to live to love and how to love to live, we must first learn about the three celestial beings that God Almighty created before He created the world, nature, and other living creatures, including Mankind. These are the Angels, Cherubim and Seraphim and the roles they played in the creation, downfall and salvation of Mankind as well as to the roles they continue to play today and until the end of the world. We will also learn. the answer as to why they were created in the first place. So first we must ask, "Who are these heavenly beings, and why were they created?" The who and why are the easy parts to answer; the when, is a little harder. First let me say that we don't know for sure when these beings were created but it was probably before the earth was created because the *Bible* tells us that Satan, who used to be one of God's favorite heavenly beings before he rebelled, was in the Garden of Eden and that he tempted Eve, and he may have been on the planet when it was a formless wasteland full of water, and when darkness covered the abyss and a mighty wind swept over the water, This was before God said, "Let there be light" and created what we call Earth. We know that he was on the earth before Man and Woman were created. All we know about Satan's creation, and thus the creation of all other celestial beings, is that he was created before the foundations of the earth were laid by God. (Job 38: 4, 7)

The important thing to know, however, is that we understand who they are and why they were created.

1. So, let's start with the Angels shall we? The *Bible* tells us that the Angels were created to be servants of the Most High Ged, and later, when Man was created, God appointed Angels to become guardians of humans, and messengers between God and Man, and they continue to be God's messengers and guardians of believers to this day. (Psalm 91: 11, Hebrews 1: 14)

The word Angel actually comes from the Greek word, *aggelos,* which means messenger. Angels are often portrayed in art and in writings as being winged creatures, but unlike the Cherubim and the Seraphim, the *Bible* does not say whether they have wings or not but we do know that they can fly so we can assume that they do, as wings would be very useful for this purpose, no? Do Angels have bodies? The answer to this question is no because they are spirits and spirits cannot have flesh and bones bodies, and the answer can be found in Hebrews 1: 14 and Luke 24: 37-39. The *Bible* does tell us that they can appear in human form, that they can eat and drink, sleep, and otherwise act as humans. So, we can assume that God gave them the power to transform themselves into human or other form at will.

Before the Big Flood some angels saw how beautiful the daughters of man were, rebelled, became wicked, left their place in heaven, came to earth and took for wives as many of them as they wanted, had intercourse with them, and had children with them. The offspring of the sons of heaven (or angels) were called the Nephilim. They were the heroes of old, the men of renown. (Genesis 6: 1-4) But, because of their disobedience, rebellion, and their horrible sin of cohabiting with human women, God held them captive in Tartarus consigned to pits of darkness to await the Final Judgment when all wicked beings, celestial and earthly, will be cast into the eternal lake of fire along with Satan himself. (2 Peter 2: 4)

2. The Seraphim (the word Seraph is singular) are beings whose main duty is to glorify God the Father and to carry out His wishes. They are stationed above God's throne and proclaim unceasingly, "Holy, Holy, Holy is the Lord of Hosts! All the earth is filled with His Glory!" They have bodies, with faces, arms, hands feet and fingers. They have six wings on their bodies. With two wings they cover their faces and with two wings they cover their feet indicating reverence for God, the Father. They can see, hear and speak in a language or tongue people can understand when necessary. They can fly and use their hands to perform services for humans as well as for God, as indicated in their praise of God and the Seraph's service to Isaiah. (Isaiah 6: 1-9)

3. In the book of Ezekiel we find a detailed description of the Cherubim (the singular of Cherubim is cherub). Here is how the Prophet Ezekiel describes the Cherubim: Their forms are human but each has four faces and four wings. Their legs go straight down but the soles of their feet are round; they sparkle with a gleam like burnished bronze. Their faces are like this: one face is the face of a man, the second is the face of a lion, the third face is the face of an ox and the fourth face is the face of an eagle. Their faces look out on all sides, they do not turn when they move, and they move straight forward. Human hands are under their wings and they carry burning coals of fire. They travel on wheels having the sparkling appearance of chrysolite. They can move in any direction they face without veering and when the creatures move, the wheels move with them, and when the creatures are raised from the ground, the creatures are also raised with them. (Ezekiel 1:1-4) Nothing like the artists draw them on valentines and on New Year's cards, are they?

Their role is to worship and serve God to reveal His Glory to all nations, especially Israel. When the Lord ordered Israel to build the Ark of the Covenant, He ordered Moses to make the ark out of acacia wood, and to plate it with pure gold on both the inside and outside and to place the Commandments inside it. Then God ordered that a cover of pure gold and two Cherubim made out of beaten gold be made for the two ends of the cover and place them on the Ark so that their wings covered the top of the cover. (Exodus 25: 1-22)

There are Angels that worship God and attend to Him every minute of every hour, of every day without ceasing. He assigned Guardian Angels from the heavenly host to protect the chosen ones from harm and evil, and yet evil exists in the world and it is evil that causes harm to humans, whether they are of the chosen ones or not.

This evil is called Satan. So what does Satan have to do with Angels? Well, Satan used to be one of God's Angels, in fact one of God's favorite Angels until he rebelled against God. In fact, the *Bible* tells us that Satan's name was Lucifer, which means Morning Star and was of beautiful countenance and arrayed in the finest raiment and adorned in the finest jewels. It was perhaps the knowledge that he was the most beautiful of Angels that caused him to become vain and to commit the sin of pride which led to his wanting to overthrow God and take over God's reign, which led to war between the Angels loyal to God, and Satan and his allies, and thus to his defeat and ouster from heaven. And, the *Bible* tells us, he managed to entice one third of the heavenly host to join him in his nefarious scheme, and thus gain allies to help him do his dirty work. His allies, or cohorts, which were former angels, are called demons and they are just as evil as Satan. Satan and his cohorts goal and efforts are aimed at destroying souls and taking them with him to hell, as well as spreading evil all over the earth.

This is what the *Holy Bible* has to say about Satan: "Son of man, utter a lament over the king of Tyre, saying to him; Thus says the Lord God: 'You were stamped with the seal of perfection, of complete wisdom and perfect beauty. In Eden, the garden of God you were and every precious stone was your covering (carnelian, topaz and beryl, chrysolite, onyx, and jasper, sapphire, garnet, and emerald); of gold your pendants and jewels were made, on the day you were created. With the Cherub I placed you; you were on the Holy Mountain of God, walking among the fiery stones. Blameless you were in your conduct from the day you were created, until evil was found in you, the result of your far flung trade; violence was your business, and you sinned. Then I banned you from the Mountain of God; the Cherub drove you from among the fiery stones. You became haughty of heart because of your beauty; for the sake of splendor you debased your wisdom. I cast you to the earth, so great was your guilt; I made you a spectacle in the sight of kings. Because of your great guilt, your sinful trade I have profaned your sanctuaries, and I have brought fire from your midst which will devour you. I have reduced you to dust on the earth in the sight of all who should see you. Among all the peoples, all who knew you stand aghast at you; you have become a horror, you shall be no more.'" (Ezekiel 28: 12-19)

"How have you fallen from the heavens O Morning Star, Son of the Dawn! How are you cut down to the ground, you who mowed down the nations! You said in your heart, 'I will scale the heavens; I will set up my throne; I will take my seat on the Mount of Assembly. I will ascend above the tops of the clouds; I will be like the Most High.' Yet down to the nether world you go." (Isaiah 14: 12-15)

"And war broke out in heaven; Michael and His Angels fought with the dragon; and the dragon and his angel fought, but they did not prevail, nor was a place found for them in heaven any longer. So the great dragon was cast out, that serpent of old, called the Devil and Satan, who deceives the whole world; he was cast to the earth and his angels were cast out with him." (Revelations. 12: 7-12)

Many theologians and teachers of the *Bible* maintain that the first sin committed was Eve's disobedience of God's orders not to eat of the fruit of the tree of life, but from the foregoing, we can attribute the first sin to Satan's sin of pride and vanity when he became so caught up in his own beauty and self-importance that he decided to overthrow Almighty God and take over His rule. As we know, he failed but he, with God's permission, still roams the earth seeking whom he can devour, as the *Bible* says. But he has already been defeated by the death and resurrection of our Lord and Savior, Jesus Christ, as we shall see and those who have been saved will get caught up in the clouds with Him at his second coming, and taken up to His Heavenly realm where they will live forever! Oh, what a glorious day that will be!

In Chapter 4, we will learn about the Fall of Mankind and the sin that caused it. It was sin that caused The Fall but it was God's Love that redeemed us from our sins. But only those who want to be redeemed are going to enter into Glory; those who do not confess their sins and repent are going to be cast into the Lake of Fire, as the *Bible* says, along with Satan and his cohorts. My dear friend, if you want to be one of those who want to attain eternal life, you must repent and accept Jesus Christ as your Personal Lord and Savior and you will be saved. This Our Lord Jesus has promised and He is The Way, The Truth and The Life. In a later chapter you will learn what you must do to be saved if you want to be saved. The key word is "want." But first, my testimony:

3 ~ My Testimony

At this point some of you are probably saying, "Oh, what a bunch of hog wash (or worse)! What fairy tale book did he copy this from!" I know that for some of you the truth is hard to take, and I used to be one of those skeptics until I decided to give my life to Jesus for the first time. I was saved for the first time at a Catholic Cursillo in Gallup, New Mexico in 1975 or 1976 and I really fell in love with Jesus to the point that I breathed, prayed and praised Jesus 24/7. I couldn't get enough of Jesus! My subordinates at work, my co-workers, my friends and relatives were amazed at the change in me! I practically glowed and walked around with a smile on my face all day, a kind word for everyone on my lips, and I couldn't wait to help someone in need or tell anyone who would listen how much I loved Jesus. And, I loved everybody!

Until one day, long story short, Satan came to visit, tempted me, and I fell away as Catholics would say or back slid as Pentecostals call it. Before I was saved at that Cursillo, I used to be negative, critical of people, judgmental, full of anger, hatred, mistrust and disbelief, just a big old horse's patootie. After I was saved, I put the old self away and put on the new man.

But then, after El Diablo came to visit me, I became the old horse's behind I had been before and the old self came back worse than ever. Even the Lord, who loves us with a love that knows no boundaries, through the Holy Spirit said, "Enough is enough! Either you straighten out, or you can go to hell." Those words scared me, but not enough; I was too busy sinning and going through marriages to pay attention to Jesus, even though my conscience bothered me a lot.

At that point, like I said, I was in deep doo doo. My wife, who had stood faithfully and lovingly by me through some rough times, who had borne me eight beautiful children, and followed me through several states as my job took me, had divorced me, my children were disappointed and hurt in me, and I took to drinking and finally moved in with another woman twenty-one years my junior and eventually married her. That marriage lasted for almost twenty guilt ridden years (I guess God hadn't given up on me, laying a heavy guilt trip on me which lasted for almost twenty five years) when she left me because she found out she had breast cancer and wanted to spare me having to care for her until she died, or so I was told by her best friend with whom she was living (out of state) when she died.

I would have gladly taken care of her until the day she died, but she didn't allow me too. I learned all this later on after her death. I was devastated. I guess she was guilt ridden, too, because by this time she had been saved, was attending church services without fail and was even on her church's outreach teams saving souls for Jesus. And then she died. I'm sure she's in heaven now because I know that she felt sorry for her part in my falling away and for me divorcing my first wife. I know she was forgiven because one day out of the blue (this was before she had left me and after she got saved) she called my first wife (or my first ex-wife), and asked her for her forgiveness, and my first wife forgave her, as did Jesus. But even though my second wife got saved and turned her life around, I still refused to do so.

By this time, my first wife, who was a wonderful lady and the mother of my children (by now my ex-wife), and my children had joined an Evangelical-Christian Church and I saw how they and my second wife had changed; they were happy, full of joy, peace and love and I was jealous and envious, but even though they had changed and were happier than they had been since their mother and I had become estranged, I refused to change. Even my oldest son had become a pastor during this time. It took me about thirty-five years and three subsequent marriages and divorces before I began to see to see the light. Luckily, neither my ex-wife, my family or Jesus gave up on me during this tumultuous time.

Every once in a while, the Holy Spirit gave me a nudge, or maybe a kick in the patootie, and I'd make an effort to change but, like I said, I was too busy going through wives and divorces, (not that I'm proud of it) that nothing fazed me. After my fourth divorce from a gentle, kind, and loving wife, I moved to Albuquerque where I met my fifth to be wife (it wasn't). The minute I saw her, I flipped and I thought I had struck gold! She was beautiful and I thought I had won the lottery! Everything went real well between us for the first year, then for whatever reasons which I have never been able to figure out the relationship started to turn sour, became abusive, then up and down, and then it turned toxic. Finally, after three years it went out of control and like a forest fire that has burned itself out, the relationship became a pile of ashes.

It was during the third year, when our relationship was going to hell, that I injured my back and it hasn't been the same since. For the next year we tried to restore the relationship and make it work, and then it finally ended in a parting of the ways (remember I wasn't born again yet). I believe that this breakup was the turning point for me. It turned my life upside down. I was a broken man, physically, spiritually and mentally. I turned to the *Bible* for answers and then I remembered how happy my first wife and children had been when they found Jesus, and I turned to them for advice.

Instead of ridiculing and hating me, they loved me and they

helped me find my way back to Jesus who was waiting for me with open arms, like the father waiting for his prodigal son to return. I started going to a small Evangelical Christian church where I was again born again and learned what Agape love is; I asked to be baptized in the Holy Spirit, and later I asked my Christian brothers and sisters to pray that I receive the Gift of Tongues, and about three weeks later, while listening to a recording of gospel music by my daughter Sylvia and her husband, Tim, I burst out spontaneously praying and speaking in tongues! What a wonderful thing it was and is! I knew then that I had been born again, and to prove it, the Holy Spirit moved powerfully within me and filled me with such wonder, ecstasy and awe! Being born again is better than winning the lottery!

And wonderful things started happening to me! My broken heart was healed, not overnight but gradually, and I became full of joy and love for others, happiness filled my heart and I became a New Creation, a child of God. This means that anyone who belongs to Christ has become a New Person; the old life is gone, and a new life has begun! (2 Corinthians 5: 17)

So, if you, dear reader are in despair, perhaps you're suffering from a broken relationship, the loss of a loved one, an illness or incurable disease or just overwhelmed with the trials of life, do not despair; turn to Jesus, let go, and let him who is the Master Healer heal you and save you. Jesus is knocking at your door, ready to help you with anything you need. Every minute of every day Jesus is saying, "Look! I stand at the door and knock. If you hear my voice and open the door, I will come in, and we will share a meal together as friends." (Revelation 3:20)

So, open the door my friend, open it wide. Jesus is standing there with love in His Heart, tears streaming down his face, His eyes swollen shut and big bruises on His Face from the beatings He endured, the crown of thorns digging deeper into His torn scalp, with arms outspread, and the blood of the nails that held Him on that cross, dripping from the wounds on His Holy hands onto the ground, just waiting to embrace you and share His love with you. Hear Him, he's begging you to come, come into His waiting arms, and here is what He is telling us, "Come to me all you who are weary and find life burdensome, and I will give you rest. Take my yoke upon your shoulders and learn from me for I am gentle and humble of heart. Your souls will find rest, for my yoke is easy and my burden light." (Matthew 11: 28-30)

Have you ever read the poem "Footprints in the Sand" by Mary Stevenson? If you haven't, I urge you to read it at your first opportunity. It really sums up what Jesus is saying in Matthew 11: 28-30. Just go online or to your local library or bookstore and you will find it there. It's beautiful. It's a copyrighted piece and that's why I didn't include it in my book, but you can get a free copy by going on the Internet.

4 ~ In the Beginning: The Creation

Okay, now we know about love, the different kinds of love, and what love can do in our lives and for us and others if we follow Jesus and His commandments. In this and forthcoming chapters, we will discover where Love comes from, when it was given to us and why it was given to us. We will begin with the Stories of Creation, why God created Mankind, The Fall of Mankind, and then in later chapters we will learn about Salvation through the Birth, Death, Resurrection, and Ascension of Jesus into Heaven, then we will learn about the Last Days, the Final Judgment and then, finally, how to learn to Live to Love and Love to Live. And why.

In the first chapter of the Book of Genesis, it says that God created the Heavens and the Earth in six days, but before we begin let me quote from 2 Peter 3: 8 which states, "But do not forget this one thing dear friends: With the Lord a day is like a thousand years, and a thousand years are like a day." So what this tells us is that a day to the Lord could be an indefinite number of twenty four hour days as we know them. Thus, a day to God could be a thousand years, a million years, or a billion years, nobody except God knows.

So, if we accept this statement of Saint Peter's to be true, we don't know if a day in the book of Genesis refers to our twenty-four hour day or to a thousand, a million, or a billion years. I think it is more plausible that one day, to God, is like a billion or a trillion years rather than twenty-four hours.

Science tells us that it took billions of years to form the earth and that it went through many changes before humans inhabited it and it's gone through a lot of changes since.

To make sure that we understand God's ways, let me quote God's Words as found in Isaiah 55: 8-9, "For my thoughts are not your thoughts, nor are your ways my ways, says the Lord. As high as the Heavens are above the earth, so high are my ways above your ways and my thoughts above your thoughts."

So now, let us begin this *Bible* narrative in the Book of Genesis, a Hebrew word meaning, "In the Beginning":

In the beginning when God created the heavens and the earth, the earth was a formless wasteland, and water covered the abyss, while a mighty wind swept over the waters. (Genesis 1: 1-2)

Then God said, "Let there be light," and there was light. God saw how good the light was and then He separated the light from the darkness. God called the light day and He called the darkness night. Thus, evening came and morning followed—the first day. (Genesis 1: 3-5)

Then God said, "Let there be a dome in the middle of the waters, to separate one body of water from the other." And so it happened: God made the dome and separated the water above the dome from the water below it and called it "the sky." Evening came and day followed—the second day. (Genesis 1: 6-8)

Then God said, "Let the water under the sky be gathered into a single basin so that the dry land may appear. Let the earth bring forth vegetation, every kind of seed-bearing plant, every kind of tree that bears fruit with its seed on it" And so it happened. God called the dry land "the earth." God saw how good it was. Evening came and day followed—the third day. (Genesis 1: 9-13)

Then God said, "Let there be lights in the dome of the sky to separate day from night. Let them mark the fixed times, the days and years, and serve as luminaries in the dome of the sky, to shed light upon the earth. "The greater one, called the sun to govern the day and the lesser one, called the moon to govern the night. Then He made the stars and set in the sky to shed light upon the earth, to govern the day and night and to separate the light from darkness. God saw how good it was. And so it happened. Evening came and morning followed—the fourth day. (Genesis 1: 14-19)

Then God said, "Let the waters teem with an abundance of living creatures, and on the earth let the birds fly beneath the dome of the sky." And so it happened: God created the great sea monsters and all kinds of winged birds. God saw how good it was, and God blessed them saying, "be fertile and multiply, and fill the waters of the seas; and let the birds multiply on the earth. Evening came and the morning followed—the fifth day. (Genesis 1: 20-23)

Then God said, "Let the earth bring forth all kinds of living creatures: cattle, creeping things, and wild animal of all kinds. And so it happened. (Genesis 1: 26) God made all kinds of wild animals, all kinds of cattle, and all kinds of creeping things of the earth. God saw how good it was. (Genesis 1: 25)

Then God said, "Let us make Man in our image, after our likeness. Let them have dominion over the fish of the sea, the birds of the air, and the cattle, and over all the wild animals and all the creatures that crawl on the ground." (Genesis 1: 26) Then the Lord God formed man out of the clay of the ground and blew into his nostrils the breath of life, and so man became a living being. (Genesis 2: 7)

Then the Lord God planted a garden in the east and He placed there the Man He had formed. Out of the ground the Lord God made various trees grow that were delightful to look at and good for food, with the tree of life in the middle of the garden and the tree of the knowledge of good and bad. (Genesis 2: 8)

A river rises in Eden to water the garden; beyond there it divides and becomes four branches. The name of the first is the Pishon; it is the one that winds through the whole land of

Havilah, where there is gold. The gold of that land is excellent; bdellium and lapis lazuli are also there. The name of the second river is the Gihon; it is the one that winds all through the land of Cush. The name of the third river is the Tigris; it is the one that flows east of Asshur. The fourth is the Euphrates. (Genesis 2: 7-14)

The Lord God then took the Man and settled him in the Garden of Eden, to cultivate and care for it. The Lord God then gave Man this order: "You are free to eat from any of the trees of the garden except the tree of knowledge of good and bad. From that tree you shall not eat; the moment you eat from it you are doomed to die." (Genesis 2: 15)

The Lord God then said, "It is not good for man to be alone. I will make a suitable partner for him. "So the Lord God formed out of the ground various wild animals and various birds of the air, and He brought them to the Man to see what he would call them; whatever the man would call each of them would be its name. The man gave names to all the cattle, all the birds of the air and all the wild animals; but none proved to be the suitable partner for the man. (Genesis 2: 18-20)

So the Lord God cast a deep sleep on the Man and while he was asleep, he took out one of his ribs and closed up its place with flesh. The Lord God then built up into a woman the rib that He had taken from the man. When He brought her to the man, the man said, "This one, at last is bone of my bones, and flesh of my flesh; This one shall be called 'Woman' for out of Her Man this one has been taken." That is why a man leaves his father and mother and clings to his wife, and the two become one body. The man and his wife were both naked yet felt no shame. (Genesis 2: 21-25)

God blessed them saying, "Be fertile and multiply, fill the earth and subdue it. Have dominion over the fish of the sea, the birds of the air, and all living things that move on the earth." God also said, see, I give you every seed-bearing plant all over the earth and every tree that has seed bearing fruit on it to be your food, and to all the animals of the land, all the birds of the air, and all living creatures that crawl over the ground, I give all the green plants for food." And so it happened. God looked at everything that He had made and found it very good. Evening came, and morning followed day—the sixth day. (Genesis 1: 28-31)

Thus, the heavens and the earth and all their array were completed. Since on the seventh day God was finished with the work He had been doing, He rested on the seventh day from all the work He had undertaken. So God blessed the seventh day and made it holy because on it He rested from all the work He had done in creation. Such is the story of the heavens and the earth at their creation. (Genesis 2: 1-4)

"So," you might be asking, "Is it so important to learn the Story of Creation?" Well, since God is the Author, Creator, Designer, Engineer and Maker of everything on this universe we need to know how and why He created Mankind. He is One God, in Three Divine Persons, Father, Son and Holy Spirit, Who had no beginning and has no end, Who Always was, Is now and always Will Be, The Alpha and the Omega, the First and the Last, forever and ever, Amen. It is to God that we owe everything that we do, everything that we own, every breath that we take, every beat of our heart, the way we are, why our brains function, why our legs and arms move, why we do what we do.

We have to remember that everything that we do and the way we look, act and live we owe to Him. Not anything in our possession belongs to us, except by His Goodness and Grace. And we can use what we own, what we earn, what we inherit, our God given talents, our education and our abilities, for not only our own good, but also for the good of those less fortunate than we. This too is Agape Love, and this type of giving and sharing Is very pleasing to God. It is one of the reasons why God created Man and Woman. We can use what He gives for Good or we can use it for Evil.

God gave us one more gift when He created us: Free Will

or Freedom of Choice and this freedom of choice is what led to the downfall of Man. It is this freedom to choose that determines every action we take, every decision we make, and every word we utter. From the time we awake until the time we go to sleep, this freedom of choice along with our heart, mind, and feelings determines what we are going to do with the time He gives us.

We will see this freedom of choice at play starting with the rebellion of the Angel Lucifer who was the most beautiful of God's angels and was thrown out of Heaven along with about a third of the angels who rebelled with him and we will see it again in the Garden of Eden, when Lucifer, now called Satan appeared to Eve in the form of a serpent and tempted her, and you know what happened as a consequence. And we see it every day in our own lives, and how we use it determines what happens next. In other words, the choices we make, determine the consequences that follow. The truth of the matter is that we, or rather our brain, makes one choice after another all the time whether we are awake or asleep. Our bodies' vital organs slow down and relax when it is time to rest, but our brain does not shut down, otherwise we would die. When we die, the brain is the last of our organs to shut down. Our brain is our control center; it controls our heart beats, our breathing, and all other bodily functions. When we're awake it tells us when to eat, when to drink, when to sleep and everything we do or don't do is controlled by our brain. Along with our heart and our nerve center, it tells us when to be naughty or when to be nice, when to laugh and when to cry, when to frown and when to smile, and so on and so forth.

Our brain is like a computer always calculating, always telling us what to do and how to act. You get my drift. It is like a light switch; when you turn off the switch, the light turns off and plunges the room into darkness. I believe that the brain is where our soul or intellect, resides. The heart, on the other hand, is where our life comes from. I believe that that is where our emotions and feelings, which comprise our spirit, come from:

love, hate, joy, anger, passion, disinterest, happiness, sorrow and so on. The heart is our life center, pumping blood and oxygen to our vital organs. When the heart stops pumping life giving blood to our vital organs, the brain dies and when the brain dies, our Spirit, which is sometimes referred to as soul leaves our body and goes to a place, sometimes referred to as Purgatory or Hades to await the Final Judgment which will be done by Jesus Himself.

I believe, this is what He meant when He said, "I am the Way, and the Truth and the Life. No one comes to the Father but through me." (John 14: 6,7) You, me, them, everyone in the world whether Jew, or Christian, Buddhist, agnostic or atheist will be judged by Jesus and I know that many a non-believer if she/he can, and does, have a change of heart, and believes before or on his or her death bed, he/she will be saved. I believe that the heart is where our emotions and our feelings reside so when someone says, "he died of a broken heart" it is literally true. When the heart stops pumping life giving blood, our brain dies. And when that happens, it's, "Adios amigo" or "Hasta la vista, baby!" So you better get prepared, now, and not wait until you're on your death bed, because we don't know when or how we're going to die.

5 ~ The Fall of Mankind

The *Bible* doesn't tell us, so we don't know, how long Adam and Eve lived the perfect life in the Garden of Eden before they fell victims to Satan and to a gift from God called Freedom of Choice or Free Will. All we know is that it was after the fall of Lucifer, AKA Satan, from God's Kingdom. Satan's fall was covered in another part of this book so we can skip the gory details. All we need to know is that Satan in the form of a serpent entered the garden of Eden and tempted Eve. Remember, that Angels, whether good angels or bad angels, are spirits but they have the power to transform themselves into whatever shape or form they want and Satan as a former Angel, and certainly one of the most beautiful ones, can and does transform himself into whatever or whomever he wants. So beware of the wolf in sheep's clothing!

Here's is what the *Bible* says about the Fall of Man: Now the serpent was the most cunning of all the animals that the Lord God had made. The serpent asked the woman, "Did God really tell you not to eat from any of the trees in the Garden?" The woman answered the serpent: "We may eat of the fruit of the trees in the garden; it is only about the fruit in the middle of the garden that God said, 'You shall not eat or even touch it, lest you die.'"But the serpent said to the woman: "You certainly will not die! No, God knows well that the moment you eat of it your eyes will be opened and you will be like gods who know what is good and bad. "The woman saw that the tree was good for food pleasing to the eyes, and desirable for gaining wisdom. So she took some of its fruit and ate it; and also gave some to her husband, who was with her, and he ate it. Then the eyes of both were opened, and they realized that They were naked, so they sewed fig leaves together and made clothes for themselves. When they heard the sound of the Lord God moving about in the Garden at the breezy time of day, the man and his wife hid themselves from the Lord God among the trees of the Garden. The Lord God then asked the man, "Where are you?" The man answered, "I heard you in the garden but I was afraid because I was naked, so I hid myself." "Who told you were naked? You have eaten, then, from the tree of which I had forbidden you to eat!" The man replied, "The woman whom you put here with me-she gave me fruit from the tree, and so I ate it."

Then the Lord said to the serpent, "Because you have done this, you shall be banned from all the animals and from all wild creatures; on your belly shall you crawl, and dirt shall you eat all the days of your life. I will put enmity between you and the woman, and between you and your offspring and hers; he will strike at your head while you strike at his heel.

To the woman He said, "I will intensify the pangs of your childbearing, in pain shall you bring forth children. Yet your urge shall be for your husband and he shall be your master."

To the man He said, "Because you listened to your wife and ate from the tree which I had forbidden you to eat, cursed be the ground because of you. In toil shall you eat its yield all the days of your life. Thorns and thistles it shall bring forth to you as you eat of the plants of the field. By the sweat of your face shall you get bread to eat, until you return to the ground from which you were taken. For you are dirt and to dirt you shall return."

The man called his wife Eve, because she became the mother of all the living.

For the man and his wife the Lord made leather garments with which He clothed them. Then the Lord God said, "See the man has become like one of us, knowing what is good and bad! Therefore, he must not be allowed to take fruit from the tree of life also, and thus eat of the fruit and live forever." The Lord. God, therefore, banished him from the Garden of Eden, to till the ground from which he had been taken. When He expelled the man, He settled him east of the Garden of Eden, and He stationed the Cherubim and the fiery revolving sword to guard the way to the tree of life.

And so it came to be that Adam became a tiller of the soil and Eve became a bearer of the other children of Adam's, including Seth who was the first direct progenitor of Noah's. ancestral line. I mention this because we will be learning a lot more about Noah later.

And this is the way the Fall of Man happened. Because of the disobedience of Adam and Eve, sin entered the world bringing with it death, disease, destruction, war, and evil. So as you can see, the choices we make determine the consequences that follow. In this case, the consequence was death. Not only death of the physical body, but loss of eternal life as well. If we make good choices, good will come of them, but if we make bad choices, bad will come of them. Well, Adam and Eve made the choices of: 1) believing Satan and; 2) disobeying God and eating of the Forbidden Fruit. The result: Death. That's the bad news. "OH?" you say 'Is there good news?" You bet your patootie there's good news! And that's what we are going to find out next.

6 ~ Why God Created Humans

I remember when I was first introduced to the question, "Why did God make me?" I was in the eighth grade in Catholic School and we had to attend catechism classes. One of the questions I remember out of the old Baltimore Catechism was, "Why did God make me?" and the answer was, as I recall, very simple, very direct and very beautiful; it was, "God made me to love Him, to serve Him, and to be happy with Him in Heaven." And this sentence sums it all up, even today. No one could put it any better, right? Even little kids understood this.

According to Billy Graham, probably the greatest evangelist of modern times, and one of my heroes, in an article he wrote for *Answers Magazine*, said that God made humans so that He could have fellowship with them. It wasn't that God was lonely or that He needed us, he goes on to say, but God made us in His image so that He could shower His Love upon us so that we could share His Love with others and love Him in return. As a Triune God, that is, One God in three Divine Persons (Father, Son, and Holy Spirit), not only did the three Divinities have fellowship with one another but they also had fellowship with the other celestial beings which God Himself had created, the angels, the cherubim and the seraphim. So why did He need us? So why did He create us? The main reason is that He needs us is to help Him accomplish His plan of salvation, pure and simple. More on that later.

There are other reasons why God created Man.

After He had created the earth, trees, plants and all the creatures of the air, sky, land and sea, God said, "Let us make man in our own image, after our likeness. Let them have dominion over the fish of the sea, the birds of the air, and the cattle, and over all the wild animals and all the creatures that crawl on the ground." God created man in His image; in the divine image He created He them; male and female He created them. God blessed them saying: "Be fertile and multiply; fill the earth and subdue it. Have dominion over the fish of the sea, the birds of the air, and all the living things that move on the earth." God also said, "See, I give you every seed-bearing plant all over the earth and every tree that has seed-bearing fruit on it to be your food, and to all the animals of the land, all the birds of the air, and all the creatures that crawl on the ground, I gave all the green plants for food. And so it happened." (Genesis 1: 26-30) So from the foregoing, we learn that God created Man and Woman so that: 1) they would be fertile and multiply. and 2) have dominion of all the living things that move on the earth. And as a bonus, God gave them seed-bearing plants, and green plants for food—all they could eat! Talk about the good life, huh?

We have learned that Man and Woman were made in the image and likeness of God. So, what exactly does this mean? First of all we need to define the word image. What do you see when you gaze into a mirror or look at a photograph of yourself? You see you, right? By the same token, how do we see God, since God is a spirit and therefore invisible? Maybe we can't see God but we can feel Him. Right? We feel His Love because God is Love, Agape Love. We feel Him because He is sharing Himself with us. And so it is when we share love with one another, because we are actually sharing God. And in sharing God, we are not only showing God that we love Him, but we are actually serving Him and helping Him accomplish His Salvation Plan. So how are people going to know that you love God? They are going to know that by the way you act, the way you talk, what and how you do for others, and how you love them. And they are going to notice it by the way you look: radiant with His Radiance and shining with His Light. Because that's what we should be: a reflection of God. A beacon of God's Light. A reflection of His Love. This is what the Apostle John tells us about God's love and ours, "Beloved, let us love one another because love is of God; everyone who loves is begotten of God and has knowledge of God. The man without love, knows nothing of God, for God *is* Love. God's Love was revealed in our midst in the following way:

He sent His only Son to the world that we might have life through Him. Love then, consists in this: not that we have loved God, but that He has loved us and has Sent His Son as an offering for our sins. If God has loved us so, we must have the same love for one another. No one has ever seen God. Yet, if we love one another God dwells in us and His Love is brought to perfection in us." (1 John 4: 7-12) Yes! God is Love! And He lives in us. And if you abide in Him, He abides in you! You are begotten of God, my friend, therefore, believe in Him, trust Him, love Him with all your heart, serve Him fervently and you will be saved.

In summary, we were created to bring honor and glory to God. But how do we do this? We bring honor and glory to God when we worship Him, when we praise Him, by the way we treat and serve others, and by the way we serve Him. God knew when He created Man that people would sin, but He made them anyway simply because He wants us to love Him and be with Him in Heaven, God knew that one of His angels was going to try to overthrow Him, but He made him anyway; and God knew that He was going to have to become man in order to save us and reconcile us to Himself. But He did all this anyway because He loved and still loves us. God is Perfect Love and Love builds on Love. Therefore, every time a person is saved, God's Love is multiplied. So be a multiplier. Love everyone!

7 ~ God's Plan of Salvation

"In the beginning was the Word;
The Word was in God's presence;
And the Word was God." (John 1: 1)

"He was present to God in the beginning." (John 1: 2)

"Through Him all things came into being,
And apart from Him nothing came to be." (John 1: 3)

"Whatever came to be in Him, found Life, Life for the Light of men. The Light shines on in darkness, a darkness that did not overcome it." (John 1: 1-5)

"The Word became flesh and lived among us. And we have seen His Glory, the glory of an only Son coming from the Father, filled with enduring Love." (John 1: 14)

"God gave us eternal life. And this life is in His Son. Whoever possesses the Son, possesses Life. And whoever does not possess the Son, does not possess Life." (1 John 5: 11-12)

So what do these *Bible* verses tell us? They tell us that Jesus is One with God the Father and that as the second of the three Persons in the Trinity, He is fully God. They tell us that He has always been part of the Trinity, and that nothing that was created was created without Him. They tell us that Jesus is the Life and a light for Man; a light that can never be extinguished. They tell us that because God loved the world so much that He became incarnate; that He came down from Heaven and His Spirit covered the Virgin Mary and she conceived and gave birth to God's Son, and named Him Jesus (which means "God Saves" in Hebrew and Christ means "Anointed One" in Greek), and that because of his great and enduring Love for us, He will save the world from their sins. So God's Plan, pure and simple, is to save our sorry hides so that we don't burn in hell, and so that we can spend the rest of eternity in glorious joy with Him and all the other celestial beings. No more tears; no more hurts; no more sorrow, only Joy!

And how did all this come to be that Man fell and had to be saved through the death of God Himself? Well, first, war broke out in the heavens and Lucifer (Satan) was booted out of Heaven, and then, in a fit of anger and revenge Satan talked Adam and Eve into disobeying God, and they were made to leave the Garden of Eden. So, what was the fall-out from all this? Well, the first thing that happened was that Evil in the form of Satan entered the world. The second thing was that because of their disobedience, Adam and Eve were separated from God, they lost communion and fellowship with God, and death through sin came to them, but don't despair; there is hope.

The Prophet Isaiah tells us that "The hand of the Lord is not too short to save, nor his ear too dull to hear. Rather, it is your sins that separate you from God and make Him hide His face and not hear you." (Isaiah 59: 1-2) The Apostle Paul in Romans 5: 18 tells us that, "To sum up, then: just as a single offense brought condemnation to all men, a single righteous act brought all men acquittal and life. Just as through one man's disobedience all became sinners, so through one man's obedience all shall become just." (Romans 5: 18-19) So salvation comes down to this: Jesus Christ. The Birth, Life, Death and Resurrection of Jesus Christ is God's Plan of Salvation for us.

So, it all comes down to these questions: What do I choose, Heaven or Hell? Whom do I wish to serve, God or Satan? "Choose this day whom you will serve. As for me and my House, we will serve the Lord." (Joshua 24: 15) Salvation is a free gift, it has already been paid for by Jesus' death on the cross, but we must want it. But merely wanting it is not going to cut it. True, it is a free gift, but we must earn it. And in order to earn it, we must serve God first. It is a free gift but can we earn it?

Okay, sounds easy enough doesn't it? But is it? Well, I'm going to give you God's Instructions on how to Live to Love, Love to Live and you can decide for yourself what you *choose* to do. It's all a matter of *choice, desire, and doing.* Anybody can say, "Sure! I want to do it!" and then go off on their merry way and forget about it. But if you have the *desire* to serve God, then you have answered the two previous questions. And the Holy Spirit, if you ask for His help, will provide the *doing*, for nothing is impossible with God.

But before I show you the way to Live in order to Love and how to Love in order to Live eternally, I'm going to teach briefly about His Birth, His Life, His Death, and His resurrection and what it means to us. And now, just a reminder that Jesus is alive and well and has been since before the world was formed, I would just like to mention that Jesus, although not mentioned by the name Mary gave him, is present to us in the Old Testament and mentioned over three hundred times. He was present as part of the Triune God at the creation of the world, the fall of mankind, after the fall, and all the other important events that happened in Old Testament times. And then we find Him again, incarnated as a human being and as savior, through His crucifixion, death and resurrection from the dead, and given the name Jesus, which means, "God Saves." But before we get into the rest of the story, let's find out who Jesus was as a man, who His ancestors were, what nation they came from and why they were chosen as his people. But first, we need to find out what happened after the fall of mankind.

8 ~ The Destruction of the Earth

There were eight generations between Adam and Noah when the Lord saw how great man's wickedness was upon the earth, and how no desire that his heart conceived was ever anything but evil. He regretted that He had made man on the earth and his heart was grieved. So the Lord said, "I will wipe out from the earth the men whom I have created, and not only the men but also the beasts and the creeping things, and the birds of the air, for I am sorry that I made them." (Genesis, chapter 6)

But God loved Mankind too much and Noah found favor with the Lord. He was a good man and blameless in that age for he walked with God. He had three sons: Shem, Ham, and Japheth. (Genesis, chapter 6) So great was God's love for humanity that He decided to spare Noah and his family so that could fulfill His Plan of Salvation.

When God saw how corrupt the earth had become, he said to Noah, "I have decided to put an end to all mortals on earth; the earth is full of lawlessness because of them. So I will destroy them and all life on earth." Make yourself an ark of gopherwood, put various compartments in it, and cover it inside and out with pitch. This is how you shall build it: the length of the ark shall be 300 cubits, its width 50 cubits, and its height thirty cubits. Make an opening for daylight in the ark, and finish the ark a cubit above. Put an entrance on the side of the ark, which you shall make with bottom, second and third decks. I, for my part, am about to bring the flood upon the earth, to destroy everywhere all creatures in which there is a breath of life; everything on earth shall perish. But with you I will establish my covenant; you and your sons, your wife and your sons' wives, shall go into the ark. Of all the other living creatures you shall bring two into the ark, one male and one female, that you may keep alive. Moreover, you are to provide yourself with all the food that is to be eaten and store it away that it may serve as provisions for you and all your household for you alone in this age have I found to be truly just. Of every clean animal take with you seven pairs, a male and its mate, and of the unclean animals, one par, a male and its mate. Thus, you will keep their issue alive over all the earth. Seven days from now I will bring rain down on the earth for forty days and forty nights, and so I will wipe out from the surface of the earth every moving creature that I have made. Noah did just as the Lord had commanded him. (Genesis, chapters 6 and 7)

Noah was six hundred years old when the flood waters came upon the earth. As the waters increased, they lifted the ark. Higher and higher rose the water until the highest mountains were submerged, and all the creatures living on the earth perished. Then the rains stopped but the waters maintained their crest over the earth for one hundred and fifty days and then God made a wind sweep over the earth and the waters began to subside. At the end of one hundred and fifty days the waters had so diminished that in the seventh month, on the seventeenth day of the month, the ark came to rest on the mountains of Ararat and the waters continued to recede. In the six hundred and first year of Noah's life, in the first month, on the first day of the month, the water began to dry up on the earth. In the second month, on the twenty-seventh day the earth was dry. (Genesis, chapters 7 and 8)

Then God said to Noah, "Go out of the ark together with your wife, your sons and their wives. Bring out with you every living thing that is with you—all bodily creatures, be they birds or animals or creeping things of the earth—and let them abound on the earth, breeding and multiplying on it." So they all came out, Noah and all his family and all the animals. Then Noah built an altar to the Lord and choosing from every clean animal and every clean bird, he offered holocausts on the altar. When the Lord smelled the sweet odor, He said to Himself, "Never again will I doom the earth because of man, since the desires of man's heart are evil from the start, nor will I ever strike down all living things as I have done. As long as the earth lasts, cold and heat, seedtime and harvest, and day and night shall not cease." (Genesis, chapter 8)

God blessed Noah and His sons and said to them, "Be fruitful and multiply and fill the earth. Dread fear of you shall come upon all the animals of the earth, the birds that move in the air, upon all the creatures that move on the ground and all the fishes of the sea: into your power they are delivered. Only flesh with its lifeblood still in it shall you not eat. For your own lifeblood, too, I will demand of it an accounting: from every animal I will demand it, and from man in regard to his fellow man I will demand an accounting for human life. If anyone sheds the blood of man, by man shall his blood be shed. For in the image of God has man been made." (Genesis, chapter 9)

God said to Noah and to his sons with him, "See, I am now establishing my covenant with you and your descendants after you and with every living creature that was with you and came out of the ark. My covenant is this: that never again shall all bodily creatures be destroyed by the waters of a flood; there shall not be another flood to devastate the earth. And this shall be a sign that I give for all ages to come: "In the sky after a rainfall, I will place a rainbow of many colors as a sign to all humans, and all living things as a reminder of the promises I made through the covenant I made with Noah." And, so it is and shall be until this earth passes away.

Noah lived three hundred and fifty years after the flood. His whole lifetime was nine hundred and fifty year and then he died. (Genesis, chapter 9)

The Dispersion of Noah's Descendants After The Flood and the Forming of the Israelite Nation

The descendants of Noah are listed in Genesis, chapter 10. It is a list of the descendants of Noah's sons Shem, Ham, and Japeth that were dispersed by God into what we know now as Europe, Asia, Africa and other parts of the world excepting the Western Hemisphere known as North, Central, and South America which became known as the New World. Before the dispersion, which occurred after the flood, the whole world spoke the same language, using the same words. While men were migrating in the east, they came upon a valley in the land of Shinar (ancient Sumer in Southern Mesopotamia) and settled there.

Then they said, "Let's build ourselves a city and a tower with its top in the sky, and so make a name for ourselves, otherwise we shall be scattered all over the world." The Lord came down to see the city and tower that the men had built. Then the Lord said, "If now, while they are one people, all speak the same language, they have started to do this, nothing will ever stop them from doing whatever they presume to do. Let us then go down there and confuse their language, so that one will not understand what another one says." Thus, the Lord scattered them from there all over the world and they stopped building the city. That is why it was called Babel, because there the Lord confused the speech of all the world. It was from that place that He scattered them all over the world. Thus, the world became populated with different peoples and speaking different languages. (Genesis, chapter 11)

In this narrative, however, we are concerned only with Shem, the first-born son of Noah since through his line comes our salvation, being that he was the father of Terah, who was the father of Abram, who was selected by God as the first Patriarch of the Israelite Nation and later re-named Abraham by the Lord, God. And because he was chosen by God, it is through Abraham and his descendants the we have our salvation. God spoke to Abram and told him, "Go forth from the land of your kinfolk and from your father's house to a land that I will show you. I will make of you a great nation and I will bless you. I will make your name great so that you will be a blessing. I will bless those who bless you and curse those who curse you. All the communities of the earth shall find blessing in you."

Abram went as the Lord directed him. Abram was seventy-five years old when he left Haran. He took his wife, Sarai, his brother's son, Lot, all the possessions they had accumulated, and the persons they had acquired in Haran, and they set out for the land of Canaan, the land the Lord had given him as far as the sacred place at Shechem. Abram built an altar there to the Lord who appeared to him, and said, "To your descendants I will give this land." From there he moved to the hill country east of Bethel. He built an altar there to the Lord and invoked Him by name. (Genesis, chapter 12)

Then Abram journeyed by stages to the Negeb where he and Lot decided to separate and go in different directions because their herds and possessions were so great that the land could not support them if they stayed together. So Abram said to Lot, "If you prefer the left, I will go to the right. If you prefer the right, I will go to the left." Lot, therefore chose the whole Jordan plain and went eastward. Abram stayed in the land of Canaan. After Lot had left, the Lord said to Abram, "Look about you, gaze to the north and south, set forth and walk about in the land, through its length and breadth, for to you I will give it." Abram moved his tents and went to settle near the terebinth of Mamre, which is at Hebron. There he built an altar to the Lord. (Genesis, chapter 13)

The Covenant With Abram

Abram and his wife, Sarai, were advanced in years when sometime after these events, this word of the Lord came to Abram: "Fear not Abram! I am your shield; I will make your reward very great." But Abram said to the Lord, "O Lord God, what good will your gifts be when you have not seen fit to give me an heir and my wife and I remain childless? I have no heir except the steward of my house." Then the word of the Lord came to Abram, "No, that one shall not be your heir. Look outside and count the stars if you can. Just so shall your descendants be." Abram put his faith in the Lord, who credited it to him as an act of righteousness. The Lord then asked for a sacrifice from Abram of a three-year-old heifer, a three-year-old she goat, a three-year-old ram, a turtledove and a young pigeon to seal the promise He had made him. When the sun had set and it was dark, a smoking brazier and a flaming torch passed between the pieces of the sacrifice he had cut up. This is the covenant that The Lord made with Abram, " To your descendants I give this land, from the Wadi of Egypt to the Great River (the Euphrates), the land of the Kenites, the Kennizzites, the Kadomites, the Hitites, the Perizzites, the Rephaim, the Amonites, the Canaanites, and the Jebusites." (Genesis, chapter 15)

And so it happened.

The Birth of Ishmael

Sarai was barren and had borne no children to Abram. She had, however, an Egyptian maidservant named Hagar. Sarai said to Abram, "The Lord has kept me from having children and I am past the child bearing stage. Why don't you have intercourse with Hagar and perhaps I shall have sons through her." So Abram had intercourse with her and she became pregnant. When she became pregnant with Abram's child, Hagar looked on Sarai with disdain. So Sarai said to Abram, "You are responsible for this outrage against me!" Abram then told Sarai, "Your maid is in your power. Do to her whatever you please." So Sarai abused her so much that Hagar ran away. The Lord's Messenger found her by a spring in the wilderness and asked her what she was doing. "I am running away from my mistress, Sarai," she replied. But the Lord's Messenger told her to go back and submit to her mistresses' abusive treatment. "I will make your descendants so numerous that they will be too numerous to count," the Lord's Messenger told her. "You shall name him Ishmael for the Lord has heard you and answered you." Hagar bore Abram's son and Abram named him Ishmael. Abram was eighty-six years old when Ishmael was born. (Genesis, chapter 16)

The Covenant of Circumcision, the Promise to Give Abram a Son by Sarai, and the Renaming of Abram and Sarai

When Abram was ninety-nine years old, the Lord appeared to him and said, "Between you and me I will establish my covenant and I will multiply you exceedingly. My covenant with you is this: you are to become the father of a host of nations. No longer will you be called Abram; your name shall be called Abraham, for I am making you the father (Patriarch) of a host of nations. I will render you exceedingly fertile; I will make nations of you; kings shall stem from you. I will maintain my covenant with you and your descendants throughout the ages as an everlasting pact, to be your God and the God of your descendants after you. I will give to you and your descendants the land on which you are now staying, the whole land of Canaan, as a possession: and I will be their God. On your part, you and your descendants after you must keep my covenant throughout the ages. This is the covenant that you must keep: every male among you must be circumcised. Circumcise the skin of your foreskin and that shall be the mark of the covenant between you and me. Every male among you including your servants and slaves, shall be circumcised. As for your wife, do not call her Sarai; her name shall be Sarah. I will bless her, and I will give you a son by her. Him also will I bless; he shall give rise to nations, and rulers of people shall issue from him, and you shall call him Issaac. I will maintain my covenant with him as an everlasting pact, to be his God and the God of his descendants. As for Ishmael, I will bless him and make him exceedingly fertile. He shall become the father of twelve chieftains, and I will make of him a great nation. But my covenant I will maintain with Isaac, whom Sarah will bear to you by this time next year." And Abraham did as God commanded him to do. (Genesis, chapter 17)

The Birth of Isaac and the Banishment of Hagar and Ishmael

Sarah became pregnant and bore Abraham a son in his old age at the time God had promised and Abraham named him Isaac. When his son was eight days old, Abraham circumcised him as God had commanded. Abraham was a hundred years old when Sarah bore him a son and Sarah was eighty-six. Isaac grew and on the day of the child's weaning, Abraham held a great feast. One day Sarah noticed that the son her Egyptian maidservant had borne to Abraham was playing with her son, Isaac and she grew angry and demanded of Abraham, "Drive out that slave and her son! No son of that slave is going to share the inheritance with my son. Isaac!" Abraham was distressed for he loved both of his sons. But God told him, "Don't be distressed about the boy or your slave woman or about the demands of Sarah, no matter what she is asking of you, for it is through Isaac that descendants shall bear your name. As for the son of the slave woman, I will make a great nation of him also, since he too is your offspring."

So Abraham, with a heavy heart, banished Hagar and Ishmael into the wilderness where he grew up, and God was with him. He lived in the wilderness of Paran and became an expert bowman. His mother got a wife for him from the land of Egypt. (Genesis, chapter 21) And Ishmael's wife bore him twelve sons who became twelve chieftains of as many tribal groups. Thus, he became the father of the Arab nations. The span of Ishmael's life was one hundred thirty-seven years and then he died and was taken to his kinsmen. The Ishmaelites ranged from Havilah-by-Shur, which is on the border of Egypt, all the way to Asshur. (Genesis, chapter 25)

The Death of Sarah

The span of Sarah's life was one hundred and twenty-seven years and then she died. Abraham buried his wife, Sarah, in the cave of the field of Machpelah, facing Mamre (that is Hebron) in the land of Canaan

The Death of Abraham

Abraham married another wife after the death of Sarah and had a son, Jacob, who became patriarch after Isaac and married a woman whose name was Keturah. She bore him six sons, However, Abraham deeded everything that he owned to his son, Isaac by Sarah, and to his other sons by Keturah he made grants while he was still living, and he sent them away eastward to the land of Kedem, away from Isaac. The whole span of Abraham's life was one hundred and seventy-five years, and then he breathed his last, dying at a ripe old age after a full life, and he was taken to his kinsmen. His sons, Isaac and Ishmael, buried him in the cave of Macpelah next to his wife, Sarah. After the death of Abraham, God blessed his son Isaac and made him the next Patriarch of the Israelites. Isaac's son, Jacob, then became patriarch after Isaac, and so the line of Jesus' ancestors continued until Jesus. You can find a list of Jesus' ancestors in Matthew 1: 1-17.

Jesus, therefore, is descended from Abraham who is known

as the first Patriarch of the Israelite people through his son, Isaac, who was born to him and his wife Sarai in their old age, and on to Jacob. Abraham is also the patriarch of the Arab peoples, and thus of the Muslims, through his son, Ishmael, who was born to Abraham and his wife's servant, Hagar.

Part Three

9 ~ Jesus' Life and Ministry

This part is all about Jesus, Our Lord, Redeemer and Savior of the world.

Jesus' Birth Foretold

So the Father, who knows all, sees all, hears all and is All, decided to put His Plan of Salvation into action and become human like us and save us out of His great love for us.

There are many prophecies concerning the birth of the Messiah or Jesus Christ, the Savior of the World found in the Old Testament, The word Jesus, which comes from the Hebrew word, Yeshua, or the Latin Jesu, means God Saves and the Words Christ or Messiah mean The Ministry of Anointed, or Chosen One. The word Messiah is of Jewish origin, and the word Christ, or Christos in Greek, comes from the Latin Christus.

Although there are more than 500 *Bible* verses regarding the birth, death, resurrection and ascension into Heaven of Jesus, I will list only some of the more relevant ones in this book. Here are some prophecies concerning His Birth that have been fulfilled:

1. He would be descended from the Patriarch Abraham and would bless all the nations of the world. (Genesis 12: 3)
    Fulfilled (Matthew 27: 50)

2. He would be a prophet like Moses. (Deuteronomy 18: 15, 17)
3. He would be born of a virgin. (Isaiah 7: 14),
   Fulfilled (Matthew 1: 19-21, Luke 1: 26-35)
4. He would be born in Bethlehem. (Micah 5: 2),
   Fulfilled (Matthew 2: 1-7, Luke 2: 4-7)
5. He was to be preceded by a messenger. (Isaiah 40: 3, Malachi 3: 1)
   Fulfilled (Matthew 3: 1-3)

That, then, is a list of some of the relevant prophesies concerning the Birth of our Savior, Jesus Christ, or Yeshua, if you want to call Him by that name. I would like to urge you to read the above referenced *Bible* verses concerning this, one of the most important and momentous events to have happened in human history. His coming, his short earthy ministry, and certainly, His death, resurrection and ascension into Heaven turned this sinful world upside down and continues to do so to this day and will continue until He comes again in glory to judge the living and the dead, and gather His Elect into His Kingdom, which will have no end.

The Genealogy of Jesus

The genealogy of Jesus can be found in two places in the New Testament: in Matthew 1: 1-17 and in Luke 3: 23-38. Matthew's genealogy of Jesus starts with the Patriarch, Abraham, or forty-two generations from Abraham to Jesus, while Luke's genealogy starts with God, to Adam, then from Adam to Jesus, or seventy-seven generations. I haven't been able to find out why the discrepancies exist, if they are discrepancies, but the only explanation I can think of is that Matthew is only counting the generations from Abraham because of the destruction of all living creatures, including the generations of people from Adam to Noah by God through the flood. As you recall, God spared Noah, and his family as the only people worthy to be saved. Since

God chose Abraham, the great-grandson of Noah as the Patriarch (which means Father), of the Israelites, and since He chose Israel as the nation from where The Savior or Messiah would be born, it would seem reasonable to assume that the author of Matthew chose to delineate Jesus genealogy this way.

On the other hand, since Jesus is the Son of God, or more specifically, God Incarnate, it would also seem reasonable to assume that the author of Luke would choose to count the generations as starting with God. You can choose whichever you like best. I prefer Matthew's version because it was, supposedly, written by one of Jesus' own apostles. Not that I'm taking anything away from Luke, the companion of the Apostle Paul, who wrote the Gospel of Luke and the Acts of the Apostles. He was a great and meticulous writer and he did his homework according to what he said at the beginning of Luke's Gospel. Again, I would urge you to read the above-mentioned *Bible* references so as to get a better picture of the genealogy of Jesus.

The Birth of John the Baptist

Let's imagine that The Father, the Son and the Holy Spirit were relaxing in their garden one day, enjoying a good Cuban cigar and/or a cold bottle of Mexican beer (Why not? Nothing is impossible with God!), when Dad probably said something like this, "Well, guys, it's time to set the wheels in motion and get those knuckle-heads down there saved before they finish themselves off. We've waited long enough. I've given them many, many chances to repent of their sins and reform their lives, but they are still bent on doing their own thing instead of following my Commandments and Laws in spite of the great leaders like Abraham, Isaac, and Moses; Kings like David and Solomon; and, the great prophets like Isaiah, Ezekiel, and Jeremiah that I've sent them.

They have been fighting each other, killing each other, committing adultery, witchcraft, smoking dope and robbing each other blind, and all sorts of evil and disobeying the prophets and leaders I sent them, so let's save them from their folly. Jesse, I'm sorry but you will have to go down to Earth, become one of those fools down there, and die a horrible death on the cross so I can save them and bring them up here to enjoy eternity with us. What do you think about that?" And Jesus replied, "Well, dad, I'll do whatever you say. I love those buggers, too. And after I come back to take my place at your right hand, I will send Holy Spirit here to keep them in line, to be their Comforter, their Teacher, their Guide and their Helper. He, like You and Me, knows everything. He sees everything, and He hears everything. He *is* God, like us, after all!"

What Jesus was saying is, you can fool all the people some of the time, but you can't fool some of the people all the time. And you can't fool God any of the time! So what am I saying here? What I am saying is that God created us not only so we could love Him and serve Him and be happy with Him in Paradise, but also so that we could become soldiers in His Army.

"What?" you ask. "Is God at war?" Yes, of course, didn't you know that? He's been at war with Satan ever since the Archangel Michael and his Army tossed Satan and his cohorts out of Heaven, ese! So the other reason God created us, is because He wants us to earn our salvation by becoming his Warriors For Jesus. Although, Christ has already bought our salvation by his death and resurrection the Father wants us to know that salvation isn't cheap. We have to earn it by the way we live, by the way we love others, and by the way we treat each other. Comprende? So now that we know what we need to do, we might ask, "Orale, and what's in it for me?" The simple answer is: Eternal Life. Salvation. Joy. Happiness. That's what in it for us!

So why does God want to save us, anyway? We've been nothing but a big pain in the Beep, Beep for him, after all. Right? The answer to that is simple, too: It is spelled L O V E . Not just love, but Agape Love, God Himself, the Ultimate Love! The answer is found in John 3: 16, "For God so loved the world that He gave His only Son so that whoever believes in Him may not die but may have eternal life." There you have it, in Jesus' own words. He loves us so much that He sacrificed the life of His only Son so that we who don't deserve His love could have eternal life. The rest of that chapter says that God did not send the Son to condemn the world, but that the world might be saved through Him. Yes, I know, I keep repeating myself, but that's the only way to learn, through repetition, que no?

In writing about the birth of Jesus, I have to write about John the Baptist first because he was the precursor to Jesus. I chose mainly to use the Gospel of Luke because of what he wrote in chapter 1, Verse 1. However, I will be using the Gospel of Matthew as a reference as well, And now, here, in Luke's words, is what the Good Book says about the birth of Our Savior: "Many have undertaken to compile a narrative of the events which have been fulfilled in our midst, precisely as those events were transmitted to us by the original eyewitnesses and ministers of the word. I, too, have traced the whole sequence of events from the beginning and have decided to set it in writing for you, Theophilus so that your Excellency may see how reliable the instruction was that you received." (Luke 1: 1-4)

Then Luke goes on to tell us about the birth of John the Baptist and what his role will be in the life of Jesus. And here's what he says, "In the days of Herod, King of Judea, there was a priest named Zechariah of the priestly class of Abijah. His wife was a descendant of Aaron named Elizabeth." According to 1chronicles 24: 1-31, there were twenty-four priestly divisions that served in the temple at Jerusalem on a rotating basis in keeping with the precepts given them by their First High priest, Aaron, as the Lord, the God of Israel had commanded him. Then Luke goes on to say, "Both were just in the eyes of the Lord blamelessly following all the commandments and ordinances of the Lord.

They were childless, for Elizabeth was sterile; moreover, both were advanced in years."

Then, Luke says, "Once when it was the turn of Zecariaiah's class (or division) and he was fulfilling his functions as a priest before God, it fell to him to enter the sanctuary of the Lord and offer incense, an Angel of the Lord appeared to him standing at the right side of the altar of incense. Zechariah was terrified but the angel said to him, "Don't be afraid, Zeke, your prayer has been heard and your wife, Elizabeth, shall bear a son and you shall call him John for he will be great in the eyes of the Lord. He will never drink wine or strong drink, and he will be filled with the Holy Spirit from his mother's womb. God Himself will go before him in the spirit and power of Elijah to turn the hearts of fathers to their children and the rebellious to the wisdom of the just, and to prepare for the Lord a people well disposed." But Zechariah was skeptical and said, "How is this possible? I am an old man, and my wife, too is past the child bearing age?" Then the Angel said,, "I am Gabriel of God who was sent to give you the good news, but now, because you have not trusted my words, I am going to strike you mute until your son is born." And that is exactly what happened. (Luke 1: 5-25)

Shortly after this happened, Elizabeth conceived and gave birth to a son whom they named John in accordance with the instructions Zechariah had received from the Angel, Gabriel. (Luke 1: 57-66) And John grew up and matured in spirit. He lived in the desert until the day when he made his public appearance in Israel. (Luke 1: 80) When John the Baptist made his appearance as a preacher in the desert of Judea, this was his theme, "Reform your lives! The reign of God is at hand!" (Matthew 3: 1-3) It was of him that the prophet Isaiah had spoken when he said, "A herald's voice in the desert; 'Prepare the way of the Lord, Make straight His paths.'" (Isaiah 40: 3, Matthew 3: 3)

Announcement of the Birth of Jesus

Six months after Elizabeth became pregnant with John, the Angel Gabriel was sent by God to Nazareth, a town in Galilee to a virgin named Mary, who was engaged to a man named Joseph, who was a descendant of King David, who was a descendant of Abraham. Mary, too, was of the House of David. Upon arriving, the angel said to her, "Rejoice, O highly favored daughter! The Lord is with you! Blessed are you among women! "Gabriel could see that Mary was troubled by his words so he said, "Don't worry, Mary, God has found favor with you and you are to bear a son and give him the name Jesus."

Mary said, "Wow! How can this be? I'm not even married yet?" Gabriel said, "Don't worry, Mary, the Holy Spirit will come upon you, and the power of the Most High God will overshadow you; hence the Holy Offspring to be born will be called Son of God. Know that Elizabeth, your kinswoman, has conceived a son in her old age; she who was thought to be sterile is now in her sixth month of pregnancy, for nothing is impossible with God." Mary said, "I am the servant of the Lord. Let it be done to me as you say." (Luke 1: 26-38)

When Mary told Joseph what the Angel had told her, he became upset and thought she was lying to him. He wanted to break off the engagement (wouldn't you) but the Angel of the Lord appeared to him in a dream and said, "Joseph, son of David, have no fear about taking Mary as your wife. It is by the Holy Spirit that she has conceived this child. She is to have a son and you are to name Him Jesus because He will save His people from their sins." (Matthew1: 18-23)

When Joseph awoke he did as the Angel directed and received her into his home. (That is, he married her.) He had no relations with her at any time before she bore a son whom he named Jesus. (Matthew 1: 25) Shortly thereafter, Mary set out into the hill country to the town of Judah to visit Elizabeth and Zechariah. When Elizabeth heard Mary's greeting, the baby in her womb leaped for joy! Elizabeth who was filled with the Holy Spirit cried out in a loud voice, "Blessed are you among women, and blessed is the fruit of your womb! But who am I that the mother of my Lord should come to me? The moment your greeting sounded in my ears, the baby leapt in my womb for joy! Blessed is she who trusted that the Lord's words to her would be fulfilled!" (Luke 1: 39-45)

Mary remained with Elizabeth for about three months and then she returned home to await the birth of her son, the Messiah, Jesus Christ. (Luke 1: 56)

John's Way of Life, and His Ministry

After the birth of John, Zecariah, his father, filled with the Holy Spirit, uttered this prophecy concerning John, "And you, O child, shall be called prophet of the Most High, for you shall go before the Lord (meaning Jesus) to prepare straight paths for Him, giving His people a knowledge of salvation, in freedom from their sins. All this is the kindness of our God." (Luke 1: 67, 76)

The child matured in spirit. He lived in the desert until the day when he made his public appearance in Israel. (Luke 1: 80) His clothing was made of camel's hair and he wore a leather belt around his waist, and his food was grasshoppers and wild honey. (Matthew 3: 4)

John was about 20 or 22 when he begin his ministry. His primary mission was to announce the coming of Jesus and to baptize those who wished to be baptized. God spoke to John in the desert and he went about the entire region of the Jordan preaching the Good News about the Messiah and proclaiming a baptism of repentance and the forgiveness of sins of sins and great crowds came out to be baptised by him in the Jordan as they confessed their sins. (Luke 3: 2-5, 6) " I baptize you in water (this is called the Water Baptism) but there is one to who is to come after me who is mightier than I (talking about Jesus). I am not fit to loosen his sandal strap. He will baptize you in the Holy Spirit and in fire." (This is called the Holy Spirit Baptism.) (Luke 3: 16) This was his theme, "Reform your lives! The reign of God is at hand!" It was of him that the Prophet Isaiah had spoken. (Isaiah 40: 3)

The Birth of Jesus

It so happened that just before Jesus was born, the Emperor Caesar Augustus issued a decree ordering a census of the whole world. So everyone went to register, each to his own town. And so Joseph went from Nazareth in Galilee to Judea, to David's town of Bethlehem to register because he was of the lineage of David, with Mary, his wife who was with child. (Luke 2: 1-5)

They probably traveled by donkey with a caravan of people who were also going to Bethlehem to register, and it probably took them five to seven days to get there. When they got there, they couldn't find a room at any of the inns, and I imagine Mary was very tired by then and ready to give birth, so she had to give birth to Jesus in a stable, wrapped Him in swaddling clothes, and laid Him in a manger full of hay. (Luke 2: 6-7) Hopefully, they found a room after the rest of the people who had come to resister for the census left, and stayed there for the period of Mary's confinement according to the law given to Moses by God. According to this Law, when a woman gives birth to a boy, she shall be unclean for seven days with the same uncleanness as her menstrual period.

On the eighth day the boy's foreskin is circumcised, and then she is to spend thirty-three more days in becoming purified of her blood. She cannot touch anything sacred nor enter the sanctuary until the days of her purification are fulfilled. (Leviticus

13: 2-6) They probably did because it says in Luke 2: 21 that when the eighth day arrived for the circumcision, the name Jesus was given to the child, the name the angel had given her. However, Mary still had to be confined for thirty-three more days! Ladies, aren't you glad you're not under the Law anymore? Now you can have your baby, get waited on by nurses in crisply ironed, white uniforms, get a good night's sleep, take a nice, hot shower in the morning and go home the day after the baby is born!

In the meantime, right after the birth, Mary and Joseph had visitors. There were some shepherds in that region, living in the pastures and keeping night watch over their flocks by turns. The Angel of the Lord appeared to them and announced the good news of the birth of the messiah. "You will find him in Bethlehem lying in a manger and wrapped in swaddling clothes," said the angel. Suddenly there appeared a multitude of the heavenly host, praising God and singing, "Glory to God in high heaven, peace on earth to those on whom His favor rests!" When the angels had returned to heaven, the shepherds hastened to Bethlehem to see for themselves this event which the angels had told them about. They found the stable which was being used by Mary and Joseph, and saw the baby Jesus lying in the manger. The shepherds returned to their fields glorifying and praising God for all they had seen.

Presentation of Jesus in the Temple

After Mary's period of confinement and purification were over, Mary and Joseph took the Baby Jesus to Jerusalem so that He could be presented to the Lord for it is written in the Law of the Lord when He said to Moses, "Consecrate to me every first-born that opens the womb among the Israelites, both of man and beast for it belongs to me." (Exodus 13: 2) And so it was done.

The Visitation of the Astrologers

After the birth of Jesus, which occurred during the reign of King Herod, some astrologers from the east arrived in Jerusalem asking, "Where is the new-born king of the Jews? We saw His star at it's rising in the east and we have come to pay Him homage." At this news, King Herod was very alarmed and disturbed; he didn't want a king for the Jews; he was the king and he would tolerate no other!

King Herod summoned all the Chief Priests and Scribes and asked them when and where this new King of the Jews was born. "In Bethlehem!" they told him. He then asked the astrologers to get detailed information about the child and to report back to him as he, too, wanted to go pay homage to the child. After their audience with the king, they set out, still following the star until it came to a stop where the child was. On entering the house, they found Mary and the Child. They prostrated themselves and did him homage. After they had done this, they presented Him with their gifts of gold, frankincense and myrrh. They received a message in a dream not to return to Herod so they went back to their homes by another route.

The Flight Into Egypt

After the astrologers had left, the Angel of the Lord appeared to Joseph in a dream and commanded him to get up, take the mother and child and flee to Egypt. "Stay there until I tell you otherwise. Herod is searching for the Child to kill Him." Joseph got up and took the Child and His Mother and left that night for Egypt where they stayed until after the death of Herod. (Matthew 2: 13-15) This fulfilled what the Prophet had said, "Out of Egypt have I called my Son." (Hosea 11: 1)

The Slaughter of the Innocents

Once Herod realized that he had been deceived by the astrologers, he became furious and ordered that all boys two years and under in Bethlehem and the surrounding area be killed. What was said through Jeremiah the Prophet was then fulfilled: "A cry was heard at Ramah, sobbing and loud lamentation: Rachel bewailing her children, no comfort for her, since they are no more." (Matthew 2: 16-15, Jeremiah 31: 15)

Return to Nazareth

After Herod's death, which occurred not too long after the Holy Family fled to Egypt, the Angel of the Lord once again appeared to Joseph in a dream, and told him that it was now safe to go back to Israel as Herod was dead. So once again Joseph took his little family and moved back to Nazareth in Galilee, which fulfilled what was said by the prophets, "He shall be called a Nazarene." (Matthew 2: 19-23) The Child grew in size and strength, filled with wisdom, and the Grace of God was upon Him. (Luke 3: 40)

The Finding of Jesus in the Temple

As good Jews and members of the Temple, Joseph and Mary used to go every year to Jerusalem for the Feast of Passover (Pesach in Hebrew) which is the Jewish Feast celebrating the exodus from Egypt and the Israelites freedom from slavery. (Exodus, chapter 12) When Jesus was twelve, they went to Jerusalem as was their custom.

As they were returning home after the festival, Jesus stayed behind unknown to his parents. Thinking He was with relatives or friends in the large party, they continued their journey. At the end of the day, not finding him among the party, Mary and

Joseph returned to Jerusalem in search of Him. On the third day, they found Him in the Temple among all the teachers, listening to them and asking questions. All who heard Him were amazed at His intelligence and His answers. When His parents saw Him, they were relieved and happy, but His mother said, " Son, why have you done this to us? Can't you see how worried we were? Your father and I have been searching for you in sorrow!" Jesus said to them, "Why did you search for me? Did you not know that I had to be in my Father's House?"

He went home with them then and was obedient to them. His mother, in the meantime, kept all these things in her heart and memory. Jesus, for his part, grew steadily in wisdom and age and grace before God and men. (Luke 2: 41-52) And, I imagine, he got into mischief like all growing boys do once in a while, and got spanked, too. But maybe not, considering. And, if Joseph was like all fathers, he probably taught Jesus some of his carpentry trade. I also imagine that the family had a few sheep for food, and that it was one of Jesus' responsibilities to care for them. I base this on Jesus' knowledge of sheep, and on His calling Himself the Good Shepherd. (John 10: 11, 14) Even David called Jesus Lord and Shepherd. (Psalm 23) And He is a really, really Good Shepherd. The best.

Jesus Prepares for His Public Ministry

Jesus' Baptism: After all the people who came from Galilee were baptized, Jesus too was baptized by John. After Jesus was baptized, he came directly out of the water, and the skies opened and the Holy Spirit of God descended like a dove and hovered over Him. With that a voice from the heavens said, "This is my beloved Son in Whom my favor rests." (Matthew 3: 16)

The Temptation of Jesus: Then Jesus was led into the desert by the Holy Spirit to be tempted by Satan. He fasted forty days and forty nights, and afterward He was hungry. The tempter approached Him and said to Him, "If you are the Son of God, command these stones be turned to bread." Jesus replied, "Not by bread alone does man live, but by every word that comes out of the mouth of God."

Next the devil took him to the Holy City, set Him on the parapet of the Temple, and said, "If you are the Son of God, throw yourself down. Scripture has it: He will bid His angles to take care of you, with their hands they will support you that you may never stumble on a stone." Jesus also answered him, "Scripture also has it: 'You shall not put the Lord, your God to the test'."

The devil then took Jesus up to a very high mountain and displayed before Him all the kingdoms of the world in their magnificence, promising, "All these will be yours if you prostrate yourself in homage before me." At this, Jesus said to him. "Away with you, Satan! Scripture also has it, "You shall do homage to the Lord, your God, and Him alone shall you adore." At that the devil left Him, and Angels came and ministered to Him. (Matthew 4: 1-11)

The Ministry of Jesus

And now we come to the public ministry of Jesus Christ, true God and true Man, Who Is, and Was, and always Will be. Although His ministry only lasted three years, He turned this old world upside down, and it never will be the same again. Never in the history of the world had there ever been such miracles performed; never had there been such preaching; never had there ever been such Love shown for mankind! Never had there been, or will there ever be, such teaching! Never has there ever been another Man like Jesus!

Jesus taught, and preached in the Holy Spirit, and He healed and heals still, by the power of the Holy Spirit. And by His teachings He inspires everyone: men, women, and children of all ages and both sexes to love, honor and obey God and one another and to forgive others as He forgives us our trespasses. And, most important of all, Jesus Saves!

And we, too, can be like Jesus, and Jesus wants us to be like Him. He wants us to love one another as He loved us; as He still loves us. (John 15: 12) In fact, when the Pharisees, in an attempt to trip Him up asked Him, "Teacher, which commandment of the law is the greatest?" Jesus answered, "You shall love the Lord, your God with all your heart, with all your soul, and with all your mind. This is the greatest and first commandment. And the second is like it, "You shall love your neighbor as yourself. On these two commandments the whole law is based and the prophets as well. (Matthew 22: 36-37)

On another occasion, a lawyer stood up to pose Him this question, "Teacher, what must I do to inherit everlasting life?" Jesus replied, "You shall love the Lord with all your heart, with all your soul, with all your strength, and with all your mind. And your neighbor as yourself." (Luke 10: 25-27) "But who is my neighbor?" you might ask. Well, I want you to take your *Bible* and open it to Luke 10: 28-37 and read it for yourself. This is the story about a Jew who was going from Jerusalem to Jericho who was beaten, robbed and left half-dead. Several people passed him by without helping him until a Samaritan came by and helped him. This point is important to note because the Jews and the Samaritan were enemies. You'll get the picture after you read the parable for yourself. And this story illustrates how Jesus also loves everybody, sinner and non-sinner alike. So we, too, must love as Jesus loves. I will be talking more about love and about how much God loves us later on in the book. After all, love is what this book is about.

After He had been preaching, teaching, and healing the people for a time, He decided to start forming His church, and like a good manager, He decided to pick his Assistants. Only He called them Apostles, and, like a good boss He delegated certain duties, responsibilities and His powers to each of them. A good boss always delegates, and Jesus is the Boss of Bosses. A good Boss always wants continuity for his organization to go forward after He leaves.

And so Jesus picked His subordinates very carefully and assigned different levels of authority according to each of their talents and experience.

One as He was walking along the Sea of Galilee, he observed two brothers, Simon now known as Peter, and His brother Andrew, casting a net into the sea. He called out to them and said: "Come after Me and I will make you fishers of men." They immediately abandoned their nets and followed Him. He walked along further and caught sight of two more brothers, also fishermen, James, Zebedee's son, and John. He called them, and immediately they abandoned their boat and their father and followed Jesus. (Matthew 4: 18-22)

Then He went out to the mountain to pray, spending the night in communion with God. At daybreak, He called together His disciples (the word disciple means a follower or student of a certain person in authority such as the disciples of Jesus) and selected the rest of them whose names were, Phillip and Bartholomew, Matthew and Thomas, James, son of Alpheus, and Simon, called the Zealot, Judas , son of James, and Judas Iscariot, who turned traitor. (Luke 6: 12-16)

After His encounter with Satan, Jesus, filled with the Holy Spirit, returned to Galilee to preach, teach, save, heal and perform other miracles, like bringing the dead back to life. He taught in their synagogues, proclaimed the Good News of the Kingdom of God, and cured the people of every disease and illness. As a consequence of this, his reputation spread throughout the length and breadth of Syria. They brought to Him all those afflicted with all kinds of diseases and racked with pain, the demon possessed, the lunatics, the junkies, the alcoholics, thieves, prostitutes, the deformed, the lepers and the paralyzed; even the dead. He cured them all.

The answer to the question "Who is my neighbor?" can be found in Luke 10: 28-37 to show us that we must love everyone, even our enemies. The reason why this parable is so important, is because in Jesus' time, the Jews and the Samaritans were enemies. There is another parable that Jesus taught that speaks of a father's love for his son and the act of forgiveness and reconciliation. This, too represents how God forgives us our sins, no matter what they are, if we confess and repent of our sins. This is the Parable of the Prodigal Son and can be found in Luke 15: 1-31.

This parable teaches us three lessons: 1) the Love of a father for his lost son, which can be compared to God's Love for us sinners; 2) the act of forgiveness, which always precedes the act of love, and; 3) the act of celebration and reconciliation at the return of the prodigal sinner.

Another example of love and forgiveness can be found in Luke 15: 1-7. This parable is about the shepherd who loses one of his sheep and takes the remaining ninety-nine sheep, puts them in the corral, and goes to look for the lost sheep. When he finds the lost sheep, he put it over his shoulder and, in jubilation sets off for home. When he arrives at home, he invited all of his neighbors and relatives to come and celebrate with him because he found his lost sheep. "I tell you," Jesus said, "there will likewise be more joy in heaven over one repentant sinner than over ninety-nine righteous people who have no need to repent." (Luke 15: 7)

The moral of these parables is: Jesus loves you friend; He forgives you your sins if you repent, and He invites you to the party He has planned for you! Eternal Life. Bienvenidos! Welcome! There are many more parables of love, forgiveness and repentance that I could show you, but I want you to read the Gospels for yourself and find out how you, too, can learn to live to love and love to live. Eternally.

Jesus also taught by preaching to the great crowds who

followed Him. He taught in the synagogues, by the seashore, on the mountains, in the desert, anywhere where people gathered to hear Him preach, and perform miracles, such as healing the sick, lame, blind and lepers. One of His greatest teachings is a blessing to the anewim (a Hebrew word meaning the poor or the disadvantaged, the needy, the poor, those in need of the spiritual blessings promised by God. called the Beatitudes, or blessings to the anewim, or the poor and needy of Jesus' day and are part of His Sermon on the Mount. (Matthew 5: 1-12)

The rest of the Sermon is a teaching on how we are to live our lives, such as how to control our anger, avoid occasions of impurity, against divorce, not to make false promises, loving our enemies, how to pray. forgiving others, fasting, how to store up heavenly treasures instead of earthly treasures, avoiding judgment, how to ask God for answers to our prayers and an admonition on how to treat others. (Matthew 5: 13-48, and all of chapters 6 and 7) Please read these three chapters. It is all there. They will change your life.

I will briefly re-cap all the important points contained in chapters 6 and 7: 1) Do not divorce, if possible, unless it's for cause like infidelity. It is a hard thing. It can cause a lot of hurt and grief to all parties concerned; 2) Do not make any false promises or oaths. Say 'yes' when you mean yes and 'no' when you mean no; 3) Forgive others their trespasses. If you forgive others, your Heavenly Father will forgive you yours. If you don't forgive others, neither will your father forgive you yours; 4) D not hoard all your earthly riches. They could get stolen. Store up Heavenly treasures instead. And don't worry about your livelihood. God will provide; and 5) Ask, and it will be given to you. Seek and you will find. Knock and it shall be opened to you.

Another time, coming down from the mountain with His disciples, He stopped at a level stretch where a large crowd of people awaited Him who had come to hear Him preach, get healed of their diseases, and get exorcised of their demons. And here is what He taught, "To you who hear me, I say: Love your enemies, do good to those who hate you; bless those who curse you and pray for those who maltreat you. When someone slaps you on one cheek, turn and give him the other one; when someone takes your coat, let him have your shirt as well. Give to all who beg from you. When a man takes what is yours, do not demand it back. Do to others what you would have them do to you." (Luke 6: 27-31)

Then He goes on to say, "Be compassionate, as your father is compassionate. Do not judge, and you will not be judged. Do not condemn, and you will not be condemned. Forgive, and you will be forgiven. Give and it shall be given to you. Good measure, pressed down, running over, will they pour into the fold of your garment. For the measure you measure, will be measured to you. (Luke 6: 36-38)

I, personally, have adopted these precepts of Jesus as my personal code of conduct. It is not easy to live by this code, but it can be done; it must be done if one is to model his or her life after Jesus. And don't get discouraged if you fail sometimes. After all, we are human, and we will backslide from time to time; but don't worry, the Holy Spirit is there to pick us up when we fall.

It takes a lot of patience and will-power, but with patience, practice, and persistence it can be done. It takes three things to accomplish your goals: inspiration, motivation, and perspiration. Like I said, it is not easy, but it can be done. It is a matter of choice. Choice and willpower. Remember: winners never quit, and losers never win. Do I sound like a motivational instructor? Maybe it's because I was one at one time.

Another thing that Jesus did to prove that He was the Messiah, sent by Father God to die as an atonement for our sins because of His and the Father's love for Mankind, was perform miracles in the Father's Name. There are at least thirty-four miracles listed in the Four Gospels of Matthew, Mark, Luke, and John, but there are many, many more miracles, proverbs, and sermons of Jesus that were not written down because, as the Apostle John (the Apostle whom Jesus loved) says in John 21: 24, there would not be room enough in the entire world to hold them all. Therefore, I will only list the most relevant ones that are applicable to the title of this book.

1. Jesus' first miracle took place at Cana in Galilee, which Jesus, Mary and some of His disciples attended. It was a big wedding, apparently, because they ran out of wine. So Mary said to Jesus, "Son, they have no more wine." And Jesus, in obedience to His Mother, and to show His disciples that He was the Messiah, ordered the servants to draw water from the well, fill six store jars with the water. They did so, and the Master of the banquet tasted the water, realized that it had been turned into wine. He was amazed! He then called the bridegroom aside, and said to him, "Everyone brings out the choice wine first and then the cheaper wine later, but you have saved the best wine until now!" This was the first of many signs He performed and His disciples believed He was the Messiah. (John 2: 1-11) The lesson here is, obey and believe. Obey Jesus' commandments, and place all your beliefs on Him, and Him alone, and you will be saved.

2. One time, when Jesus was preaching in the temple a man who was possessed by an unclean spirit stood up and cried out, "What do you want with us, Jesus of Nazareth? Have you come to destroy us? I know who you are-the Holy One of God!" "Be quiet!" Jesus said sternly. "Come out of him." The impure spirit shook the man violently and came out of Him with a shriek. The lesson: Jesus has power! He can cast out evil spirits and they are afraid of Him. So as long as we are obedient to Jesus, we need not fear evil beings for Jesus is with us.

3. Another time, a leper came to Him and begged Him on his knees, "If you are willing, you can make me clean." "I

am willing," Jesus said and reached out His hand and touched the man, saying, "Be clean!" Immediately, the man was healed. (Mark 1: 40-42) **Lesson: Jesus Heals.**

If you believe. But He heals in His own time. Sometimes He heals right away. Sometimes He makes us wait; and sometimes, we don't get healed, probably because of our lack of faith or, for whatever reason. So, too, must we pray for healings, our own and others. Sometimes He will perform a miracle and heal you, and other times He may want you to be healed by doctors; and at other times, for whatever reason only He knows, there will be no healing. Sometimes it is through our hurt, whether of body or a broken heart, that we are able to give Him thanks and praise.

4. Soon afterward Jesus went to a town called Nain and His disciples and a large crowd followed Him. As He approached the town gate, a dead person was being carried out—the only son of is mother, and she was a widow. A large crown from the town was with her. When Jesus saw her, His heart went out to her and He said, "Don't cry." Then He went up and touched the coffin they were carrying the son in and said, "Young man, I say to you, Get up!" The dead man sat up and began to talk, and Jesus gave him back to his mother. (Luke 7: 11-13) **Lesson: Jesus has compassion and can bring the dead to life.** So, too, must we have compassion on our fellow-man in order to have eternal life.

5. As Jesus went on from there, two blind men followed Him, calling out, "Have mercy on us, Son of David!" "Do you believe that I can do this?" He asked them. "Yes, Lord," they replied. Then He touched their eyes and said, "According to your faith let it be done to you." And their sight was restored. According to your faith you are healed. (Matthew 9: 27-31) **Lesson: We must not only believe, but we must have faith that whatever we seek and ask for, we shall receive.** (Matthew 7: 7) For unless we believe, we have no faith, and without faith, we

have no hope and hope is the essence of all we seek and ask for. But, one thing we must remember: Although God answers every prayer, not ever thing that we ask for may be granted; only what is for our own good, and sometimes what we ask for is not always good for us. Sometimes God says, "No." "For I know the plans I have for you, declares the Lord, plans to prosper you and not to harm you, plans to give you hope and a future." (Jeremiah 29: 11)

6. One day a friend of Jesus named Lazarus got sick, so his sisters, Mary and Martha, sent for Jesus and asked him to come immediately because His friend was dying. In spite of the urgency of the situation, Jesus waited until Lazarus had died and had been in the tomb for four days before He arrived at Mary and Martha's home intending to bring Lazarus back to life. He did this for two reasons: first, for God's glory so that God's Son would be glorified through this act, and; second, so that Mary and Martha and all those who accompanied them would believe that He was the Messiah sent to save the world.

When Martha heard that Jesus was coming, she went out to meet Him, but Mary stayed home. "Lord," Martha said to Jesus, "If you had been here, my brother would not have died." "Your brother will rise again," Jesus answered. "I am the resurrection and the life. Whoever believes in me, even though they die, will have eternal life. Do you believe this?" "Yes, Lord I believe," Martha said. Then Mary, accompanied by some Jews, all weeping, also came to meet Jesus, and He was filled with compassion. Jesus wept. And, filled with The Holy Spirit and compassion, Jesus asked that the stone be rolled away from the tomb where Lazarus was buried.

"But Lord," Martha said, "He has been in the tomb for four days, by this time there is a bad odor." "Did I not tell you that if you believe, you will see the Glory of God?" So they took away the stone, and Jesus, looking up to Heaven prayed, "Father, I thank you for hearing Me. I know that you always hear me but I said this for the benefit of the people standing here, that they may believe You sent Me." Then Jesus said in a loud voice, "Lazarus, come out!" The dead man came out, his hands and feet wrapped with strips of white linen and a cloth around his face. Jesus said to them, "Take off his grave clothes and untie him, and let him go." (John 11: 1-45) **The Lessons: 1) Jesus loves us; 2) Jesus can do anything, even raise people from the dead; 3) He has compassion for us; and 4) that nothing is impossible to God, if we believe.**

This was one of he last miracles that Jesus performed and although this miracle caused many of the Jews who had come to visit Mary and Martha during Lazarus' death, to believe that Jesus was the Messiah. But because it also caused the chief priests of the Pharisees and the Sanhedrin much anguish, and they begin to start plotting the death of Jesus. (John 11: 45-54)

This and more, was prophesied by the Prophet Isaiah when he called Him "a Man of Sorrows who suffered our infirmities, endured our sufferings, was pierced for our offenses, crushed for our sins; upon Him was the chastisement that makes us whole, and by Whose stripes we were healed." (Isaiah 53: 1-12) Please read the entire chapter.

The Last Days of Jesus

You may start your reflections on the Passion of Our Lord starting with the next sentence:

The last days of Jesus were spent teaching in the temple by day and retreating to the Mount of Olives to spend the night. At daybreak, people came to hear Him at the Temple. (Luke 21: 37-38) A few days before the Passover Festival, Jesus and His Disciples had decided to come to Jerusalem for a series of discourses concerning the Divinity of Jesus, His role as the Messiah, His Death, Resurrection and Ascension into Heaven, and His coming once again in Glory to judge the living and the dead. A great crowd awaited Him waving palm branches and shouting for joy and praise, as Jesus entered Jerusalem riding on a donkey. (John 12: 12-19)

After He had finished His series of discourses He declared to His disciples, "You know that in two days time, it will be Passover, and that the Son of Man is to be handed over to be crucified." (Matthew 26: 1-2)

These discourses can be found in John 14: 1-31, 15: 1-27, 16: 1-33, 17: 1-26. I strongly urge you to read and meditate on these passages before you proceed to the Part Four. This will take some time, I know, so you could break the session up into two days by reading "The Last Days of Jesus" and the "Discourses" the first day, and "The Sorrowful Passion of Jesus" the next day. Or you can skip the Discourses and read them privately another time. Whatever suits you. (But continue reading.)

Also, at this time, the Chief Priests and elders of the people were gathered at the palace of the Chief Priest whose name was Caiaphas plotting to arrest Jesus and kill Him, but not during the festival for fear of a riot among the people. (Matthew 26: 3-4) Then, one of the Twelve Disciples, Judas Iscariot by name went up to the priests and asked, "What are you willing to give me if I hand Him over to you?" They paid him thirty pieces of silver and from that time on Judas looked for an opportunity to hand Jesus over. (Matthew 26: 14-16) Jesus knew that His time on earth was almost over and that He would soon be with His Father in Heaven, leaving the Holy Spirit in charge. See John 14: 26, 15: 13.

Part Four

10 ~ The Sorrowful Passion, Death and Resurrection of Jesus

The Passover (Also Known as The Feast of the Unleavened Bread)

The Jewish Passover Festival was near which meant that many people from the country would go to Jerusalem for Passover purification. (For a full description of this Festival you may refer to Exodus, chapter 12. For a full understanding of how and why this Festival came to be, you need to read Exodus chapters 7 through 11.) This is another great example of God's love for His Chosen People and all Mankind.

This festival is also called The Feast of the Unleavened Bread. On the first day of the feast the disciples asked Jesus where He wanted them to prepare the Paschal lamb. He said to them, "Go to this certain man in the city and tell him, 'Our Master said to tell you that He wishes to celebrate Passover with His apostles at your house.'" The disciples did as they were told and prepared the Passover Meal. (Matthew 17-19)

Before they ate, the Paschal meal, Jesus realized that the hour had come for Him to pass from this world and return to the Father. He had loved His disciples while in the world and He would show His love for them until the end. The devil had already induced Judas to betray Him, so he took off His cloak, put a towel around His middle, poured water in a pan, and, in spite of Peter's loud protests, washed His apostles' feet. After He had washed their feet, he put His cloak back on, and reclined at table.

"Do you understand what I just did for you?" He asked them. "You call me Teacher and Lord, and fittingly enough for that is what I am. But if I washed your feet, I. who am Teacher and Lord, then you must wash each other's feet. What I just did was give you an example: as I have done, so must you do." (John 13: 1-17)

When it grew dark, He reclined at table with the twelve. In the course of the meal He said that one of them was about to betray Him. They all wanted to know who the betrayer was and Jesus told them the one who had dipped his hand into the dish with Him was the one. Then Judas, His betrayer said, "Surely it is not I, Rabbi?" Jesus answered, "It is you who have said it." (Matthew 26: 20-25)

During the meal Jesus took bread, blessed it, broke it, gave it to His Apostles and said, "Take this and eat it. This is my Body, which will be given up for you. Then He took the cup of wine, gave thanks, and gave it to His disciples and said, "All of you must drink from it." He said, "For this is my blood, the blood of the new and everlasting covenant which is to be poured out in behalf of many for the forgiveness of sins. Do this in memory of me. I tell you, I will not drink this fruit of the vine from now until I drink it again with you in my Father's reign." Then, after singing songs of praise, they walked out to the Mount of Olives. (Matthew 26: 26-30)

The Apostles kept asking Jesus who the betrayer was. "The one to whom I give the bit of food I dipped in the dish is the one." He dipped the morsel, then gave it to Judas Iscariot. Immediately afterward, Satan entered Judas' heart and he left immediately after eating the morsel. (John 13: 25-30)

After Judas left, Jesus was talking to His Disciples and

glorifying God. "My children," He said, "I will not be with you much longer and where I am going you cannot come. I give you a new commandment: "By your love for one another, such as my love has been for you, so must your love be for each other. That is how all will know you are my disciples: your love for one another."

"Lord," Peter said to Him. "Why can I not follow you? I will lay down my life for you!" "You will lay down your life for me, will you?" Jesus answered. "I tell you truly, the cock will not crow before you have denied me three times." (John 13: 33-37)

Then Jesus held his last discourse with His Disciples before He died. (I want you to read this discourse for yourselves, John, chapters 14, 15, 16, and 17. You will be glad you did. I want you to start getting in the habit of reading The Word of God daily.) Jesus said, "Not on bread alone is man to live but on every utterance that comes from the mouth of God." (Matthew 4: 4)

(And for those who are not Catholic, or whose church does not incorporate The Stations of the Cross as part of their Easter Services, you're more than welcome to use this version or another version as part of your Easter Services. Or if you want to attend a Lenten service where they celebrate The Passion of Our Lord, you may want to inquire at any Roman Catholic, Eastern Orthodox, or Greek Orthodox Church for the Traditional Service or a Lutheran or Anglican Communion church for the Station of the Cross for Protestants.)

Jesus' Last Hours, His Death and Burial

And now that we have celebrated the Paschal meal, listened (read) and meditated with Jesus and His Apostles, and walked to the Mount of Olives with them, we are going to be with Our Savior in His last hours on earth as He prays and agonizes in the Garden of Gethsemane, which is in the Mount of Olives, and be with Him and His apostles as He is arrested, tried and found guilty (even though He is the most innocent of men). And as we walk each Station of The Cross with Him, we will watch as He is whipped, crowned with thorns, stoned, beaten, spit upon, speared on His side as He becomes the most abused of men as He walks, carrying His own cross, on the Way of Sorrows to Calvary where he is crucified and gives up His life for our sins; and where He forgives us at the end; proof that there is no greater Love than to give up one's life for one's friends.

We will watch and sorrow with Mary, His Mother, and all those who were there as He says, "Father, forgive them. They do not know what they do!" We will experience the earthquake, the period of darkness when the sun ceased to give its light, and the rending of the Temple curtain in two which is a sign of the New and Everlasting Covenant which He promised His disciples when they partook of His Body and Blood during the First Holy Communion at the Last Supper.

And now it is time to experience The Passion of our Lord Jesus Christ as He is arrested, falsely accused, sentenced to death, tortured, and abused, and finally crucified, died and buried. He did this all because He loves us and wants us to be saved so that we can experience the joys of Heaven with Him for eternity.

So take a break, stretch your body, use the bathroom if you have to, get a cup of coffee and a biscochito (New Mexican cookie) and prepare yourselves to walk the Via Dolorosa with Him. You can do this devotion as a group, or individually as you wish. I prefer doing this devotional with a group, like in a Church Service.

Opening Prayer: "Father, may we, sinners though we are, experience Your Love and the Power of the Holy Spirit, at this moment and at every moment during this life, and may we be found worthy to enter into Your Kingdom when we pass on to the next life. In Jesus Holy Name. Amen."

Now, open your *Bibles* and recite "The Stations of the Cross for Catholics and Non-Catholics," also called "The Scriptural Way of the Cross" and also "The Scriptural Stations of the Cross." It is a devotional inaugurated by Blessed Pope John Paul the Second on Good Friday in 1991 for use by both Catholic denominations and non-Catholic denominations. I like to recite the following prayers before and after each Station, and you are welcome to do so as well: You can find the Gospel's name, chapter number and verse number next to the title of the reading.

Before Each Station:

LEADER: We adore You, O Christ and we Bless You.
ALL: Because by Your Holy Cross you have redeemed the world.

After Each Station:

ALL: Lord Jesus, help us walk in your steps.

The Stations of the Cross for Catholics and Non-Catholics:

1. Jesus' Agony in the Garden   (Matthew 26: 36-41)
2. Jesus is Arrested   (Mark 14:43-46)
3. Jesus is Condemned by the Sanhedrin   (Luke 22: 66-71)
4. Jesus is denied by Peter   (Matthew 26: 69-75)
5. Jesus is judged by Pontius Pilate   (Mark 15: 1-5, 15)
6. Jesus is scourged, and crowned with thorns   (John 19: 1-3)
7. Jesus bears the Cross   (John 19: 6, 15:17)
8. Jesus is helped to carry the Cross
       by Simon, the Cyrenian   (Mark 15: 21)
9. Jesus meets the women of Jerusalem   (Luke 23: 27-31)
10. Jesus is Crucified   (Luke 23: 33-34)
11. Jesus promises His Kingdom
       to the Repentant Thief   (Luke 23: 39-43)
12. Jesus speaks to His Mother

and the beloved disciple   (John 19: 25-27)
13. Jesus dies on the Cross
          and is placed in the Tomb   (Luke 23: 44-46)
14. Jesus is placed in the Tomb   (Matthew 27: 57-60)

To Be Recited After Readings:

LEADER: We adore You O Christ and We Bless You
ALL: Because by Your Holy Cross you have redeemed the
World. Amen.

The Traditional Stations of the Cross

    Although some say that the Traditional Stations of the
Cross started with Saint Francis of Assisi, Catholic friar, deacon,
preacher and founder of the Franciscan Order of Friars, Minor
who was born circa 1181and died in 1226, the Traditional
Stations of the Cross are a Fourteen-Step Catholic Devotional
that commemorates Jesus' last days on earth as a man, and are
attributed to Saint Alphonse Liguori, a Catholic Bishop, spiritual
writer, composer, musician, artist, poet, lawyer, scholastic
philosopher, and theologian who was born on August 1, 1787 and
died on September 27, 1696.
    Whatever the case may be, the fourteen Stations of the
Cross focus specifically on events that happened on the day Jesus
was condemned to die, His journey to Calvary, His crucifixion,
death and burial, just as they are in the Scriptural version of this
devotional. This devotional is almost always celebrated indoors
in a Catholic Church and each station is recited at each station as
the participants move from one station to the next as they read
from the *Bible* or booklets containing the stations and prayers

applicable to the stations. You can usually find pictures, or wooden carvings of the traditional stations hanging on the inside of the outside walls of a Catholic Church.

The only Stations of the Cross that I've seen prayed outside of a church are those of a Morada (Chapter) of the Hermanos Penitentes (Penitent Brothers) of which there are still some active chapters in parts of Southern Colorado, New Mexico, Arizona and Texas in the United States and South America. My experience with the Penitente Brotherhood is covered in my book, *Mi Vida Loca*.

In the Penitente Service, which is held outdoors during the afternoon on Good Friday, the stations, (descansos or resting places), made of wood, cement, or large boulders are placed along a path representing the Via Dolorosa or The Way of Sorrows, fourteen in all and each one represents a different Station where the elderly or infirm can rest while prayers are said and hymns sung while waiting to move on to the next station with the thirteenth and fourteenth stations usually located in front of the Oratorio (Chapel) where the tinieblas part of the service (the darkness which fell over the earth at Christ's crucifixion), will be held next.

The devotional procession is led by the Hermano Mayor (Head Brother), followed by the pitero (flute player), rezadores (prayers), cantadores (singers). The rest of the Hermanos (Brothers) and anyone who wants to participate in praying and celebrating this devotional come next. The Penitente Brotherhood is composed of Catholic Laymen and has its roots in Spain. It is a benevolent and charitable organization that served as a substitute church in places where there were no ordained clergy available to serve the colonists of New Mexico and Southern Colorado.

Whether you like the traditional Stations of the Cross better than the Stations of the Cross for Protestants and Catholics, or vice versa, and even on whether you participate in either of the devotionals, the important thing we need to understand

and remember is that God loved us so much that He willingly sacrificed His son as a ransom for our sins, and we need to recognize the great sacrifice Jesus made by willingly allowing Himself to be tortured to the point of death and then giving His life for us so that our sins may be forgiven again, and again, and again!

Do you understand what Jesus has done for you, for me, for all? Do you understand the value of this great gift God has given us? What does this gift mean to you, to me, to us all? It means Eternal Life. No more pain. No more sorrows. No more shame. No more worries. Only joy, love, happiness, bliss, forever and ever. Are you willing to **Live to Love, Love to Live**? If you are, now is the Day of Salvation. Don't wait another day, another hour or another minute. Do it Now! Give your all to Him, because He has given His All for you. And if you get the chance, you should see the movie *The Passion of the Christ* and/or read *The Dolorous Passion of Our Lord Jesus Christ* by Anne Catherine Emmerich.

My dear friend, don't wait until Lent to "Get right with God." Get right with Him right now. Repent. Confess your sins to Him even though He knows what they are, how many there are, and how many more there are going to be, because He sees all, hears all, knows all and is all.

And here's what you have to do:

1. Examine your conscience; have remorse for what you've done.
2. Repent. Resolve not to commit the same sin(s) again.
3. Ask for forgiveness from the person(s) you have offended, sinned against, or sinned with.
4. Confess your sins and ask Jesus to forgive you.
5. Say the following prayer and you will be saved and/or forgiven.

"My Dear Jesus, I know that I am a sinner. I want to turn away from my sins, and I ask for your forgiveness. I believe that you are the Son of God, that you died for my sins, and that you were raised from the dead and ascended into heaven to sit at the right hand of the Father. I want you to come into my heart and take control of my life. And I want to follow you as my Lord and Savior from this day forward in Jesus' (Name) Amen."

And you don't even have to say penance! He has done it all for you. He has paid the penalty for your sins by His Precious Shed Blood. If you feel like you have to do penance for what Jesus did for you, do something good for someone in need. Instead of praying one Our Father and ten Hail Marys as a penance, do something nice for someone. If you see someone in need of a smile, give him one of yours; if you see someone without shoes, give him yours, if they fit, or buy him a pair. And throw in a couple pairs of socks and some foot powder! If you see someone in sorrow, cry with him. If you see someone hungry, buy him a loaf of bread and a package of baloney; then buy him a fishing rod and teach him to fish. Or, better yet, help him find a job.

If you confess with your mouth that Jesus is Lord and believe in your heart that God raised Him from the dead, you will be saved. (Romans 10: 9) And if you've prayed the Sinner's Prayer, and have believed, you are forgiven and saved right now.

"For all have sinned and fall short of the Glory of God." (Romans 3: 23) No one is perfect; we all sin, so don't criticize; praise instead. You can catch more flies with honey than you can with vinegar.

And Jesus said, "I have come that they may have life, and have it more abundantly." (John 10: 10) He came so that we may have eternal life and enjoy fellowship with Him in Heaven.

Jesus' Resurrection and the Women at the Tomb:

After the Sabbath, as the first day of the week was dawning, Mary Magdalene came with the other Mary to inspect the tomb.

Suddenly there was a mighty earthquake as the angel of the Lord descended from Heaven. He came to the stone, rolled it back, and sat on it. In appearance he resembled a flash of lightning and his clothes were as white as snow. The guards were paralyzed with fear of him and fell down like dead men. Then the angel addressed the women and said, "Do not be frightened. I know you are looking for Jesus, the crucified, but He is not here. He has been raised exactly as He promised. "Come and see the place where He was laid. Then go quickly and tell the disciples, 'He has been raised from the dead and has gone ahead of you to Galilee, where you will see Him.' That is the message I have for you." They hurried away from the tomb, half-overjoyed, half-fearful, and ran to carry the good news to His disciples.

Suddenly, Jesus stood before them and said, "Peace!" The women came up and embraced His feet and did Him homage. At this, Jesus said to them, "Go and carry the news to my brothers that they are to go to Galilee, where they will see me." (Matthew 28:1-10)

Jesus Appears to the Disciples and Delegates His Authority to Them

The Great Commission. The eleven disciples made their way to Galilee, to the mountain to which Jesus had summoned them. At the sight of him those who had entertained doubt fell down in homage. Jesus came forward and addressed them in these words: "Full authority has been given to me both in Heaven and on earth: go, therefore, and make disciples of all nations. Baptize them in the name of the Father, and the Son and the Holy Spirit. Teach them to carry out everything which I have commanded you. And know that I am always with you, until the end of the world!" (Matthew 28: 1-20) Even though the disciples had locked the door to the place where they were staying, Jesus came and stood before them and said, "Peace be with you" and showed them His hands and His side. "Peace be with you!" He said again, "As the

Father has sent me, so I send you." Then He breathed on them and said, "Receive the Holy Spirit. If you forgive men's sins, they are forgiven; if you hold them bound, they are held bound."

So what did Jesus do here? Again, He delegated the power and authority which had been given to him by the Father, not only to baptize and make converts of all men and women, but to forgive their sins. They, in turn, delegated the same authority to their successors until the present day. (John 20: 19-23)

Gone Fishing. The "boys," Simon Peter, Thomas (the twin), Nathanael (from Cana in Galilee), Zebedee's sons, and two other disciples had decided to go fishing. All through the night, they caught nothing. Just after daybreak Jesus was standing on the shore, though none of them recognized Him.

"Hey, camaradas!" (comrades) Jesus shouted, "did you catch anything?" He asked. "No, nada, man," Peter replied. "Not even a cold!" "Cast your nets to the starboard, Jesus suggested. So that's what they did and they caught so many fish, the net was about to break. Then they recognized Jesus and Peter threw on some clothes (he was naked) and he and the disciple who Jesus loved, jumped in the water and swam to shore. The other disciples came in the boat towing the net full of fish. When they landed, they saw a charcoal fire with a fish on the grill and some bread by the side. "Bring some of the fish you caught," Jesus told them, "and grill them. Let's chow down, man, I'm hungry!" They caught a hundred and fifty sizable fish in that little while and the net was not even torn! "Come and eat your meal, guys," Jesus said. This was the third appearance Jesus had made to the disciples since being raised from the dead. (John 2: 114)

Simon Was Named Peter and Head Apostle

When Jesus came to the neighborhood of Caesarea Philippi Jesus asked His Apostles, "Who do people say that the Son of Man is?" they replied, "Some say John the Baptizer, others Elijah, still others Jeremiah or one of the prophets." "And you, who do you say that I am?" "You are the Messiah," Simon answered. "Blessed are you, Simon son of Jonah!" Jesus said. "No mere man has revealed this to you except my Heavenly Father. I for my part declare to you: you are Rock and on this Rock I will build my church and the gates of hell shall not prevail against it. I will entrust to you the keys of the kingdom of Heaven. Whatever you declare bound on earth, shall be bound in Heaven; whatever you loose, shall be loosed in Heaven."

Thus, He made Peter the Head or Chief Executive Officer of His physical Church on earth. (This was before His passion.) (Matthew 16: 13-20) Next, after His Passion when he appeared to His Apostles on Lake Tiberias and performed the miracle of the fishes, He entrusted the rest of his Apostles to Peter's care, and here's what happened: When they had eaten, Jesus sat down with his crew and addressed Himself to Peter. "Simon, son of John, do you love me more than these?" "Yes, Lord. You know that I love you," said Peter. "Feed my sheep," Jesus replied. A second time, Jesus asked, "Simon, son of John, do you love me?" "Yes Lord, you know that I love you!" Jesus replied, "Tend my sheep." A third time, Jesus asked him, "Simon, son of John, do you love me?" Peter was hurt (and probably a little annoyed, knowing Peter's temper) so he replied, "Lord, You know everything. You know very well that I love you!" Jesus said to him "Feed my lambs. (John 21: 15-17)

At this point some of you are going to say, Oh no! Here we go again with that Pope business. That's not what Jesus called Simon!" You're right, He called him shepherd; but isn't that what a shepherd is to his sheep: a papa, a daddy, a dad? And isn't that what the word Pope means, a papa, a daddy, a dad. Jesus did tell His disciples that the Father would send the Paraclete, or Holy Spirit in His name and that the same Holy Spirit would instruct them in everything and remind them of all that Jesus told them. That would make the Holy Spirit General Manager or

Big Papa? (John 14: 26) So doesn't that make the Holy Spirit the Big Shepherd over the entire Flock then? Of course, it does, and Jesus is the Bigger Shepherd! Nobody is or should be disputing that. Jesus Himself sent the Holy Spirit to bear witness on His behalf and to guide them to all truth. (John 15: 26, 16: 13) But didn't Jesus appoint Peter as the shepherd of His flock? And who is Jesus' flock? All believers are Jesus flock! And if one of his flock gets lost, doesn't a good shepherd put the rest in the corral and goes in search of the one lost sheep? Or does he leave it out there for the coyotes to munch on? And. didn't He Himself say He was the Good Shepherd? (John 10: 10) So it stands to reason that Jesus didn't want His flocks to get scattered so He put one Shepherd, speaking through and for the Holy Spirit, in charge of the other eleven so that they wouldn't be going astray.

One flock instead of twelve; isn't that what Jesus wanted? One catholic (universal) church instead of twelve anonymous ones? And so, this is the way it should be today: one united, universal church instead of so many different denominations calling each other names. It doesn't matter what you call yourself, Catholic, Episcopalian, Baptist, Presbyterian, Methodist, Mormon, Evangelical, Pentecostal, as long as we recognize each other as Christian, loving one another as Our Savior commands us to do, forgiving one another our trespasses, taking care of the needy, the infirm, the sick and the sorrowing, doing charitable works instead of evil works. In other words, **Living to Love and Loving to Live Eternally.**

Conclusion

It is the same apostle, the one whom Jesus loved, who is a witness to these things. It is he who wrote them down and his testimony, we know, is true. There's still many other things that Jesus did, that if written down in detail, I doubt there would be room in the entire world to record them. (John 21: 24-25)

Jesus' Final Instructions to His Apostles and His Ascension Into Heaven

Like the Gospel of Luke, the Acts of the Apostles was written by the physician Luke who was a traveling companion of the Apostle Paul. Paul played a major role in the formation and establishment of the Christian Church and the spread of Christianity throughout the then known Christian world. Saul, as Paul was known before his conversion, was a member of the Jewish Priesthood dedicated to the eradication of Christians. He carried letters from the Jewish priests authorizing him and his companions to arrest and bring to Jerusalem any man or woman found living according to the new Christian way, wherever and whenever he encountered them. But Jesus had other ideas, as we shall see.

Luke's narrative is addressed to Theophilus, which means Beloved by God, and could have been addressed to a person, or to the whole Church He freely admits, though, that he was not an eyewitness, but that he endeavored to interrogate as many eyewitnesses as possible to arrive at an accurate account of Jesus' life, death, resurrection and ascension into heaven after having first instructed the apostles He had chosen through the Holy Spirit. And here is what Luke has to say in the First Chapter of Acts about the events which followed Jesus' ascension. After his suffering, death and resurrection, Jesus appeared several times over the course of many days, speaking to them about the reign of God. On one occasion when He met with them, He instructed them not to leave Jerusalem. "Wait rather for the fulfillment of my Father's promise, of which you have heard me speak. John baptized with water but within a few days you will be baptized with the Holy Spirit. You will receive power when the Holy Spirit comes down on you, then you are to be my witnesses throughout

Judea and Samaria, yes, even to the ends of the earth."

No sooner had He said this then He was lifted up before their eyes in a cloud which took Him from their sight. They were still gazing up into the sky when two men dressed in white appeared beside them. "Men of Galilee," they said. "Why do you stand here looking up at the skies?" "This Jesus who has been taken from you will return, just as you saw Him go up to Heaven." After that, the Apostles returned to Jerusalem from the Mount of Olives to the upstairs room where they had been staying and devoted themselves to constant prayer to await the coming of the Holy Spirit Whom Jesus Himself would send to them to instruct, guide, help, empower, and counsel them and all believers to this very day.

There were some women in their company, and Mary, the mother of Jesus, and His brothers. One day, while waiting for the coming of the Holy Spirit, Peter stood up in the midst of his brothers and the other disciples of Jesus; there must have been a hundred and twenty gathered together, and said, "Brothers, the saying in Scripture uttered long ago through the mouth of David was destined to be fulfilled in Judas, the one who guided those that arrested Jesus. He was one of our number and he had a share in this ministry of ours. That individual bought a piece of land with his unjust gains, and fell headlong upon it. His body burst wide open, all his entrails spilling out. This property is known as The Field of Blood. It is fitting, therefore, that one of those of our company, who has been with us from the beginning until Jesus was taken from us, be chosen to replace the one who betrayed Him."

At that they nominated two: Joseph (also called Barsabbas) and Mattias. After praying, they drew lots and the choice fell to Mattias, who was added to the eleven. This, then, formed the nucleus of the Church founded by Jesus Christ under the power and authority of the Holy Spirit Whom Jesus Himself sent from the Father to guide them, teach them, show them, love them, help them and protect them, and He, Himself, promised to be with them until the end of time. This very same Holy Spirit resides within those who believe.

Do you believe? Do you want to believe? Do you want to be filled with the Holy Spirit? If you don't yet believe, but want to believe, seek out a Holy Spirit filled Church and become baptized in the Holy Spirit. If you don't believe me, study the Scriptures. I especially recommend that you read and thoroughly study the Gospel of John, the Book of Acts, First and second Corinthians, and the Epistles of first, second, and third John. I am not saying, don't study the rest of the *Bible*; that would be like telling you to eat your dessert first, and not the main course.

Better yet, especially if you are a newbie to the *Bible*, join a Bible Study Group, get a mentor, become a volunteer in your church or a hospital or home for the elderly, and see the difference in your life. The reason I'm urging you to read those Scriptures first, is so that you will better experience the birth pangs of the new church, the trials and tribulations that the members of the new church had to endure, and the outpouring of the Agape Love that was sown in the hearts of these newcomers by the Holy Spirit. You will also learn how the Apostle Paul, who as Saul his mission in life was to persecute the followers of Jesus, but was converted and became one of the greatest Apostles of Jesus Christ. What an inspiring story! By the time you finish reading the Acts of the Apostles and the accompanying Letters (or Epistles) to the Churches, you will want to rush outside, run to the nearest church and Shout, "Hey! You in there! I want to be baptized!"

Descent of the Holy Spirit:

When the Day of Pentecost came it found the disciples gathered in one place getting ready to celebrate the Feast of Pentecost. Suddenly, from up in the sky came a noise like a strong, driving wind which was heard throughout the house where they were staying. Tongues as of fire appeared and came to rest on each of them. All were filled with the Holy Spirit and began to express themselves in strange tongues and make bold proclamations as the Spirit prompted them.

Staying in Jerusalem for the celebration of Pentecost were devout Jews from every nation under heaven. These, too, heard the sound and assembled in a large crowd. They were very confused because each one heard the disciples speaking in his own language. "Are not all these people Galilean?" they asked. "How is it that we all hear them in our own language? What does this mean?" they asked. "We come from different countries yet each of us hear them talking in his own tongue about the marvels God has accomplished!" "Ah, they've had too much new wine to drink!" sneered another.

Whereupon Peter stood up with the Eleven and addressed the crowd with His famous discourse which you can find in Acts 2: 14-40. After Peter finished his discourse, he goes on to say, that some three thousand were converted and added to their group that day. Such is the power of the Holy Spirit, my friends. For with God, everything is possible. Peter never one who was afraid to speak up and tell it like it is, and being filled with the Holy Spirit just gave Him that much more power and authority to speak up. And the Holy Spirit can do the same with you, too.

After that, all the disciples, old and new, devoted themselves to the apostles' instruction and the communal life, to the breaking of bread, and the prayers. A reverent fear overtook them all, for many wonders and signs were being performed by the apostles. Those who believed, shared all things in common; they would sell their property and goods, and divide everything on the basis of each one's need. They went to the temple area together every day, while in their homes they broke bread. With exultant and sincere hearts they took their meals in common, praising God and winning the approval of all the people.

Day by day, God added to their number those who were

being saved. Hallelujah! Such is the power of the Holy Spirit. And what the new community of believers exhibited, was the purest form of Agape Love. And so, this is the way the church that Jesus Christ Himself founded got its start. And this is the way that Jesus wants us to love one another: in Agape Love, with Agape Love, and for Agape Love.

Are you ready to start loving with Agape Love? Good! Because here it comes! But just remember, friends, that it's not all fun and games. While there is an abundance of love, joy, peace and bliss, there will be times of tears, sorrow, pain and grief. You can't have one without the other. But, the rewards you will reap, far outweigh the pain and sorrow you will encounter, because it is only through love that all good things, especially eternal life, are achievable.

Part Five

11~ Live to Love, Love to Live

By now, you're saying, "Okay, Medardo," would you get to the point and tell us what you mean by Live to Love, Love To Live?" I will gladly do so! It simply means this: When God created Mankind, He created us in love, to love, and out of love because He is Love. The answer to your question can be found in The Great Commandment, "You shall love the Lord, your God with your whole soul, your whole heart, and your whole mind. This is the greatest commandment, and the second one is like it 'You shall love your neighbor as yourself.' On these two commandments the whole Law is based, and the Prophets as well." (Matthew 22: 36-40)

These are not empty words for God the Father Himself set **The Great Example** which we find in John 3: 16, "For God so loved the world that He gave His Only Begotten Son that whoever believes in Him may not die but have eternal life." And Jesus gives us further instructions in Luke 6: 35-38, to: "Love your enemies and do good; lend without repayment. Be compassionate as your Father is compassionate; do not judge and you will not be judged. Do not condemn and you will not be condemned. Forgive and you will be forgiven. Give, and it shall be given to you."

Then in Matthew 7: 12 He gave us the **Golden Rule**, "Treat others the way you want to be treated."

The Process:

So we finally come to the last part of the book, but just as the death of Jesus was the end of His earthly ministry, it was also just the beginning of His Church on earth and His Work of Salvation. This work of salvation is to be accomplished through His ministers, the clergy, you and me, and all believers under the guidance of the Holy Spirit Who is always with us, and His Angels who guard us and watch over us. All praise, honor, and glory be to you, Lord Jesus Christ, forever and ever. Amen.

Live to Love and **Love to Live** is a **Process**. A process involving a gift that was given to mankind from the time of the Creation of Man. This gift is called Free Will or Freedom Of Choice. Whatever you want to call it, however, it involves your will, and the type of choices you make. In other words, the choices we make determine the consequences that follow. In no instance is this statement truer than when God created Adam and Eve. He created them, and all humans, in His image as I've explained elsewhere in this book, and created a beautiful place for them to live in with all kinds of fruit and plants to eat, with the exception of the fruit from the tree of life, because, as God warned them, "You shall not eat it, or even touch it, or you will die."

Well, you know what happened: Satan, the father of lies, the great deceiver, the evil one, he who roams the world like a roaring lion seeking whom to destroy appeared to Eve and deceived her into believing that it was okay to eat it. She, in turn, deceived Adam, and he, too, ate of the forbidden fruit and so sin and death entered the world. "Just as through one man's disobedience all became sinners, so through one man's obedience all shall become just." (Romans 5: 12) And it has been so ever since in the way we use Free Will in determining the choices we make. This freedom of choice that we have can be used for good or for evil; we can use it to build up, or we can use it to tear down.

It controls everything we feel, do, think about, and dream about. It can turn us into raging lions one second or turn us into peaceful lambs the next. Everything we do involves our free will, from the time we wake up in the morning, until we go to sleep at night. With it, we make choices about what or when we eat, sleep, wake up, or work. With it we can make a choice whether we stop at McDonald's or Starbuck's for coffee on the way to work.

The question is: is our conscience, and therefore our Free Will, controllable or uncontrollable? It can be both, depending on many different aspects which most of us, unless we are medically trained, are not qualified to determine. Let us take the example of the coffee, a little bit further. Let's say that stopping for coffee is going to make you late, but you're free will tells you, "It's okay, man, stop and get your adrenaline going, it's only coffee. It's okay to be late." Then your conscience tell you, "No, you can't be late. Remember that deadline you have to meet?" Who are you going to listen to: your free will, or your conscience? Only you can answer that question. But, let me just say this: to a conscientious person, the conscience is going to win. That should tell you that one's free will is controllable and changeable, and it can be controlled, other than through force or chemically, only by and through our conscience.

But what is our conscience? Scientifically, conscience is a cognitive process based on an individual's moral philosophy or values system. In laymen's terms, I would describe conscience as that little inner voice that tells one when something is right or wrong. According to the theory of "Okayness," we all have three voices that tell us what to do: Our Inner Child, Our Adult, and Our Parent voices, and that we act in accordance with which voice is dominant at a particular event or time requiring a decision on our part. With some people, and particularly with those who can't control their urges and desires to do what they know is wrong, their Inner Child is the one they're going to listen to most of the time, and we all know that kids, especially if they are not taught better can get in trouble a lot. Even mature adults whose inner Child is the Dominant one is going to be a menace to society and to themselves.

Conversely, when our Parent's voice tells us, "Stop! Didn't I teach you better than that?" we say, "Yes, mommy." And we stop, right? Well, maybe unless we have a disobedient Child in control. So I hope you gather from that last statement, that the Voice we should strive to have as our dominant voice most of the time should be our Adult voice because a wise, mature, reasoning adult is more likely to make the right choice.

But I sort of deviate from the subject of Conscience. I used to teach courses based on those concepts when I was in the training business and I just couldn't resist throwing that bit in. Please forgive me. Well, we have determined that our Free will can be controllable and changeable and now the question is how do we do that, no? Well, we're about to find out. You might also call this process, a methodology for changing one's value system from negative behavior to positive behavior or changing our personality from a hateful and selfish one, to the loving and compassionate one that Jesus Himself gave us. The important thing to remember is that this concept is based on Scriptural Principles of Love and Forgiveness, or Agape Love. Since God gave His All for us, we must also be willing to give our all for one another. We can do no more, and we can do no less. That is Agape Love, and that is how we must love if we are to **Live to Love**, and **Love to Live**.

Changing and Controlling Our Free Will

Basically, the process of changing and controlling our Free Will is very simple, but not easy as you will find out. For this process to succeed, it is a matter of "Letting Go, and Letting God." It is a matter of recognizing that by yourself, you can do nothing and that with God, nothing is impossible; it is a matter of putting your whole trust and your whole life in God's hands. And above all it is a matter of Love. If you said the sinners prayer, and meant it, you're well on your way to accomplishing this process. I strongly recommend getting a mentor or mentors and a good *Bible*; it will make learning and using the process a lot easier. Some people can do it by willing themselves into doing it; most can't. But, the easiest and best way to accomplish this, and to keep you on the right track, is to join a Spirit-filled Church, (if you are not already a member of one) where you will be loved and cared for, and where everyone there is your Christian Brother and Sister. I am not recommending that you belong to any particular denomination. It can be Catholic, Protestant, Pentecostal, Evangelical, or Mormon. My only recommendation is that it be a Holy Spirit filled church, and there are Holy Spirit filled churches in every denomination, although not all are, and that's where the differences come in.

This process requires, besides a strong conscience, a lot of: 1) Will Power and Desire, 2) A lot of Repetition and Practice, 3) a lot of Concentration and Self-Awareness, 4) a lot of Love and Patience with people who irritate you, especially yourself and, 5) Developing **A Winner's Attitude**. And what is a Winner's Attitude? It is basically this: Believing in God and believing in yourself and trusting God, and trusting yourself. Remember this: a winner never loses, and a loser never wins. If you abide in Christ, and Christ abides in you, you're already a winner! Imprint that in your mind, and constantly affirm to yourself, "I am a winner! I am a winner!" Now, everybody say "I am a winner!"

I will give you a list of affirmations to practice and memorize later on. Basically, what we are doing when we learn to do something, is acquiring a new habit, which means that we acquire a new way of doing things, a new way of saying things, a new way of acting, and/or a new way of thinking. To do this, we must replace the old habit with a new habit. For example, let's say you want to stop smoking. What would you do, start chewing tobacco? No! Of course not! That would be replacing one bad habit with another bad habit! Yet, I've actually known people who have done this (including me).

The same way with quitting drinking alcohol. I knew a man who used to drink a fifth of vodka every day. Needless to say, he ended up in the hospital suffering from the aftereffects of the alcohol. The doctors told him to stop drinking vodka or he would die, so what did he do? He switched to drinking wine which eventually killed him. Replacing a bad habit with another bad habit is not the way to do it. Replacing a bad habit with a good habit is the way to do it. If you want to quit using the name of God in vain, for example, say, "God bless you!" instead! When I quit smoking, I quit cold turkey, but believe me, it wasn't easy. Sometimes the craving for nicotine was so great, I chewed my fingernails down to the very nubs. Praying helps a lot. But, besides the help of the Holy Spirit, it takes a lot of guts, repetition, self-awareness, and changing one's attitudes.

There's a lot of self-help programs out there with fancy titles like "I'm Okay, You're Okay," based on the theory of learning Transactional Analysis as a way to solve life's problems, and "Maslow's Hierarchy of Needs," based on Abraham Maslow's five step pyramid of human needs as a tool for motivating people by satisfying their human needs, starting with the basic needs for food, water, sex, shelter and safety to a person's need for self-actualization. I also used, and developed, several courses on "How to Develop a Positive Attitude," and methods such as yoga, and meditation. I taught them all, including supervision, management and human relations when I owned my Personal Training and Development business. But that was a long time ago.

They are good programs, but there is nothing, and I mean nothing like the Principles and Teachings found in *The Holy Bible* and there never has been nor will there ever be a better, more loving, more compassionate, or greater teacher than Jesus. So, for changing habits, and becoming a new creation in the Lord, stick with the Great Healer, and place all your trust in Him, and you will be changed. Find a good Spirit Filled Church and give your old life, and your old habits to Jesus and He, through the Holy Spirit, will make a New Creation out of you. And, if you aren't already filled with it, He will fill you with Agape Love so you, too, can infect others with your love as well. That's what He wants us to do, and that's what He commands us to do.

Don't get me wrong, though; I'm not advocating getting rid of doctors or hospitals. Of course, there may be, instances, including those involving drugs, alcohol, some physical and mental problems, that require medical attention, and if your case, or that of someone you know, who needs medical attention, by all means get medical help. And I'm not saying that Divine Intervention doesn't work; it does in many cases. I've personally seen people, including yours truly, being healed after being prayed over. It doesn't work in every case, and only God knows why. But even if you need medical help, don't forget to pray and thank God for His intervention and help to the physicians for their help. Miracles do happen; they happened during Jesus' ministry on earth, and they are happening today. But remember, it is only Jesus Who heals, not the person or persons laying hands on a sick person, although Jesus may use you, or me, or someone off the street as the intervenor, for His is the Power, and the Praise, and the Glory forever and ever. Amen.

As I've said above, it takes a lot of repetition and a change of habits and attitudes to change one's personality or way of behaving, so following I will give you a list of affirmations to repeat and believe in, and a list of possible attitudes you can change. It is through repetition (and making mistakes) that we learn everything: how to talk, how to walk, how to pray, how to drive, and so forth. We also learn our habits and our behavior from the people around us. If you're around people, especially parents, who drink, smoke, fight, and steal all the time, you are more than likely (but not always) to turn out to be just like them. If you're around people who are nice to each other, pray all the time, help others out and just plain love others, you are more than likely (but not always) to be like them, too. Why did I add the phrase "but not always"? Because just as there's almost always a rotten apple in every barrel, there's almost always one bad member in every family, too. Conversely, there's always a few good apples in a barrel of rotten ones, too, just as there's likely to be one good member in a bad family, no? I'm sure you know what I'm talking about, and I'm sure you've seen people change, too, just as I have. For some people changing may be instantaneous, like the Apostle Paul's conversion (although perhaps not as dramatic), while to others it may take longer, maybe even years, but if you are determined and persistent and turn your life over to God, change will happen. It's inevitable.

Affirmations

"So what is an affirmation?" you might ask. Simply stated an affirmation could be expressed in this way: An affirmation is a sentence or thought that is implanted into our subconscious mind through our conscious mind which purpose is to automatically, voluntarily or involuntarily express a strong desire and a clear mental image which is aimed at creating and bringing about a desired effect or action. The repetition of an affirmation and the resultant mental image affect the subconscious mind which in turn influences and/or changes one's behavior, habits, actions and reactions. Or, you could turn it into a form of prayer to ask the Almighty, in Jesus Name, for something that you, your church or someone you know, really need.

Here is an example of how an affirmation may be expressed:

Whatever I Ardently DESIRE,
Constantly ASK FOR,

Consistently VISUALIZE,
Fervently and Thankfully PRAY FOR,
And sincerely, BELIEVE.
Will Eventually come to PASS.

As you can see, in order for an affirmation to work, we need the following **Positive Elements** in order for it to come about: **Desire, Visualization, Prayer**, and a strong **Belief** that it will eventually come to pass. And, this requires a lot of Prayer, Patience, Belief, and a Winner's Attitude. The following are a few examples of some Affirmations I use. You may want to use these, too, and you may want to add your own to this list. The way you should express an affirmation, is as if it is already occurring, not as happening in the future. Remember: The past is already gone, and the future is not here yet. All we have is **Now** and **Now** is a **Gift**. Maybe that's why it's called the **Present**.

I am God's child, (your name,) and I have the right to exist because I was born.
I am God's child (your name,) and I exist to be great.
I am God's child (your name) and I succeed at everything good that I do with the Holy Spirit's help.

The foregoing are only examples and you don't have to state that you're God's child every time if you don't want to (it's obvious that you are), but an affirmation must be stated positively. Don't use negative words like I won't, I can't, or I should, or I'm going to. Always state your affirmation as if it's already an accomplished fact because the mind, like a computer responds to what you input—garbage in, garbage out; sweetness in, sweetness out. Do this consistently along with your morning and evening prayers. You might think this is a lot of hocus-pocus but it's Biblical truth. If you don't believe me, read Romans 12: 2 in the next paragraph.

Just like a car, the mind needs a tune-up or overhaul periodically, as does one's physical body. Good Affirmations, Partner!

The Power of the mind is very strong and like free will, it can be used for good, or for evil, so be careful how you use it. If you keep telling yourself "I'm no good!" "Nobody likes me!" "I'm stupid!" "I'm nobody!" or, if somebody told you that as a child or is telling you that now, you're more likely to carry those attitudes into adulthood, and they can be blessing, devastating, success producing, or failure producing. So **Change Your Mind To Change Your Attitude**! Tell yourself, "I Love me, I'm good, or "I'm smart, I'm beautiful" and you will be. Or you can say, "I hate myself, I'm ugly, I'm stupid, I'm a failure," and you will be. Whatever you think, you will be. You have the Power, given to you by Almighty God, to change yourself. And when others see how you've changed, they will want to change, too, and you can help them. Just **believe** in yourself, and practice what I've taught you, and you will become a New Creation in Jesus. It says so right there in 2 Corinthians 5: 17: "If anyone is in Christ, he is a new creation. The old man has passed away; now all is new!" Romans 12: 2 says "Do not conform yourselves to this world but be **Transformed** by the **Renewal** of your mind."

And the best news of all, is that you can find all you need to know on how to change and how to love from your very own copy of the *Holy Bible*. And when you learn to love, you will want to live to love, and love to live. And best of all, you won't have to spend thousands, or even hundreds of dollars to do this, **It's Free**. Jesus has already paid the price for you! So, what are you waiting for? **Now** is the Day of Salvation! Break loose from the bonds that are holding you back. Be like the Little Train that Could. Do you see how the words **Desire, Ask or Pray For, Visualize and Believe** work together to change your mind and attitudes? It's hard work, but it works. But, I have to caution you: you have to be consistent in practicing this formula, if you want it to work.

How to Forge or Restore a Relationship With Others

A relationship may be compared to a grape vine. In order to thrive and bear fruit, a grape vine requires a loving and caring vine grower, the vine, and the branches. In this comparison, God the Father is the vine grower, Jesus is the vine, and we are the branches. The grower takes care of the vine, while the vine supports the branches, and the branches bear the fruit.

However, a branch cannot bear fruit apart from the vine, and neither can a relationship thrive without Jesus and the Holy Spirit. (John 15: 1-8) This goes for all kinds of relationships, whether in the **Erotic** Stage, the **Storge** stage, the **Phileo** stage or the **Agape** stage. Relationships, like grape vines, must be fed, cultivated, and cared for lovingly if they are to survive. Although a broken and dying relationship can be difficult to restore, it can be brought back to life better and stronger than ever if we treat each other with love, kindness, and respect. God doesn't want us to get hurt or to hurt others. He wants us to love one another as He loved us. (John 15: 9-12) He has plans for each one of us, "Plans for our welfare and not for woe. Plans to give us a future full of hope." (Jeremiah 29: 11)

In addition to love, there must also be forgiveness, and the release of anger, resentment, jealousy, and envy. In other words, get rid of the LOVE KILLERS and cultivate the **Love Tillers**. So, in order to forge a good relationship, or to revive a dead or dying one, I have listed the following ways in which we can develop Positive Attitudes or habits and get rid of Negative Attitudes or habits:

Let Us Treat One Another:	Tillers	Killers
With Love, Instead of Hate	Love	Hate
With Forgiveness, Instead of Retribution	Forgiveness	Retribution
With Joy Instead of Anger	Joy	Anger
With Praise, Instead of Criticism	Praise	Criticism
With Blessings, Instead of Curses	Blessings	Curses
With Good, Instead of Evil	Good	Evil
With Embraces, Instead of Pushes	Embraces	Pushes
With Soft Caresses, Instead of Hard Blows	Caresses	Blows
With Smiles, Instead of Frowns	Smiles	Frowns
With Kindness, Instead of Harshness	Kindness	Harshness
With Encouragement, Instead of Discouragement	Encourage-ment	Discourage-ment
With Kind Words, Instead of Hurtful Words	Kind Words	Harsh Words
With Understanding, Instead of Judgment	Understanding	Judgment
With Humility, Instead of Pride	Humility	Pride
With Patience, Instead of Impatience	Patience	Impatience

And Here Is Why We Live to Love, and Love to Live:

Beloved,
Let us love one another because Love is of God.
Everyone who loves is begotten of God and has knowledge of God.
The person without Love has known nothing of God, **For God Is Love**.

God's love was revealed in our midst in this way: He sent His only Son into the world that we might have Life through Him. Love then, consists in this: not that we have loved God but that He has loved us and has sent His son as an offering for our sins.

Beloved, if God has loved us so, we must have the same Love for one another. No one has ever seen God, yet if we love one another, God lives in us, and His Love is brought to perfection in us. The way we know we live in Him and He in us is that He has given us of His Spirit.

God is love and whoever abides in Love, abides in God and God in them.
Love has no room for fear; rather, perfect Love casts out fear. And since fear has to do with punishment, love is not yet perfect in one who is afraid.

If anyone says, "My Love is fixed on God," yet hates his brother, is a liar. One who has no love for the brother he has seen cannot love the God he has not seen. The commandment we have from Him is this: whoever loves God, must also love his brother.

—Compiled from 1 John 4: 7-13, 16-21

Prayer of Affirmation and Love:

Lord, Make me an instrument of Your Peace; where there is hatred, let me sow Love;
Where there is injury, pardon; where there is doubt, faith; where there is despair, hope;
Where there is darkness, light; and where there is sadness, joy.
O Divine Master, grant that I may not so much seek to be consoled as to console; to be
Understood as to understand; to be loved, as to love; for it is in giving that we receive, it
It is in pardoning that we are pardoned, and it is in dying that we are born to eternal Life.
    —Prayer of Saint Francis of Assisi

I will now close this book with a daily prayer of thanks and praise.

Dear Lord, I give you praise for Who You are, and all that You
do. Thank You for your faithfulness.
Life may not always be good, but You are good all the time,
Please help me to put you first in all things.
Please help me to embrace your joy.
Please help me to live my life in an attitude of gratitude.
Please help me focus more on what I have than in what I lack.
Please let me focus on all that is right instead of what is wrong.
I commit this day to you and all that's in it. In Jesus' name I pray.
      Amen.

Prayer of Affirmation and Belief

The Lord is my Shepherd; I shall not want. In green pastures He gives me repose.
Besides peaceful waters He leads me, He refreshes my soul. He guides me in right paths,
For His Name's sake. Even though I walk in the dark valley, I fear no evil for you are at my
Side with your rod and your staff that give me courage.
You spread the table before me in the sight of my foes. You anoint my head with oil, my cup
Overflows. Only goodness and kindness follow me all the days of my life; and I shall dwell
In the House of the Lord forever.
    —Psalm 23

To You Be All Praise, and Thanks, and Glory, and Honor, O Almighty God.
—Happy Loving And Happy Living
Your Friend and Brother in Christ: Medardo Gonzales

For the Reader:

Themes
Describe the theme(s) of the book.

Evaluation
Make your main points here. Evaluate the book. Draw your conclusions.

Conclusion

This book was written in thanksgiving to God for saving me and all that He has done for me and mine. The theme of the book is Love and more specifically, Agape Love. It was written in Love, about Love, for Love, and for Him Who is Love. I don't know why God chose me to write this book, but I was prompted, prodded, coached, inspired, motivated, and helped by the Holy Spirit during the time I spent writing it. All thanks, honor and glory to Him in Whom we live and move and have our being. (Acts 17: 28) Thank you Jesus! Perhaps it is the turbulent times that we live in that prompted God to choose the time, place, and person to write this book and gave me the wherewithal to complete the task. Although I am unworthy of such honor, I nevertheless humbly accept the task.

I'm afraid that we're heading for the last days, for the time of the Great Tribulation and the end of the world. The signs are there in the *Holy Bible*, in the writings of the Prophets, in the Gospel of Matthew, and in the Book of Revelation. We have been warned, and unless we turn to God, Who is Love, and start loving and helping one another as He has commanded us to do, I'm afraid this country and this world are going to hell in a hand basket and those who miss the air-borne boat, jet-liner, rocket-ship, a UFO from outer space or whatever is going to carry the Elect to meet Jesus in the clouds during the rapture are going to be caught up in very, very hard times the likes of which have never been seen before, when Satan is loosed to wreak havoc during the Great Tribulation. So, for His sake, our sakes and everybody's sake, let us love one another, help one another and pray for one another, always giving thanks to God for everything and in everything, in Jesus' name.

So, my friend, are you going to be one of the raptured ones, or one of the captured ones? Your choice!

About the Author

Medardo Gonzales currently lives in Albuquerque, New Mexico. He was born on January 4, 1933 in La Jara, a small farming and ranching community nestled in the foothills of the San Pedro Mountains in Sandoval County, New Mexico, near Cuba, New Mexico. He attended school in the two-room school house which taught students from the community starting in first grade through eighth grade. His first language was Spanish and it was in La Jara Community School that Medardo learned to read, write and speak English.

In August of 1947, the family moved to Gallup, New Mexico where he enrolled in eighth grade at Sacred Heart Cathedral School, which was run by the Franciscan Order under the tutelage of Franciscan Priests and Nuns. He graduated from high school in 1952, was drafted into the U.S. Army in March of 1953, served in Korea and Japan from April 20, 1953 until April 5, 1955. He returned to Gallup where he started his Federal Government career in 1956, starting at the very bottom rung of the ladder and where he served in various administrative positions. He started as a file clerk, and he retired as an Administrative Manager in 1982.

After he retired, he worked for the Bureau of Indian Affairs Training Center in Continental Divide, New Mexico as a contract instructor specializing in course development and presentation of course materials in the areas of Supervision, Management, and Human Relations for two years until the Department of the Interior closed the Center for budgetary reasons. Following that, He worked for the University of New Mexico as a Community Development Specialist for two years. After a stint as a Community Development Specialist, he contracted with the Bill Oliver Training Corporation of Albuquerque, New Mexico and was with the corporation until the owner closed his business because of ill health.

He then opened his own training business in Gallup, New Mexico called New Horizons Training and Technical Assistance which he operated for six years until he decided to pursue other business interests, including the ownership and operation of a flower and gift shop in Grants, New Mexico. He learned all of his writing skills during his career with the Bureau of Indian Affairs, and although he wrote many, many letters, memoranda, and manuals while a federal employee, and has written short fiction books, children books, *Bible* stories, and poems for his own and his family's entertainment.

He is an avid student of the *Bible* and hopes that this book helps you to become a better person as the *Bible* has helped him. May God bless you, and may His love, peace and joy be yours forever. And I hope that before you come to the last chapter you will have learned why the book's title is **Live to Love, Love to Live**.

CPSIA information can be obtained
at www.ICGtesting.com
Printed in the USA
FFHW020646290119
50335809-55406FF

9 781632 932556